MW00998222

THE UNOFFICIAL POLDARK COOKBOOK

THE UNOFFICIAL POLDARK COOKBOOK

85 Recipes from Eighteenth-Century Cornwall, from Shepherd's Pie to Cornish Pasties

TRICIA COHEN and LARRY EDWARDS

Skyhorse Publishing

This book has not been approved, authorized, or endorsed by the British Broadcasting Corporation (BBC), Public Broadcasting Service (PBS), Winston Graham, or his publishers.

Skyhorse Publishing books may be purchased in bulk at special discounts for sales promotion, corporate gifts, fund-raising, or educational purposes. Special editions can also be created to specifications. For details, contact the Special Sales Department, Skyhorse Publishing, 307 West 36th Street, 11th Floor, New York, NY 10018 or info@skyhorsepublishing.com.

Skyhorse® and Skyhorse Publishing® are registered trademarks of Skyhorse Publishing, Inc.®, a Delaware corporation.

Visit our website at www.skyhorsepublishing.com.

10 9 8 7 6 5 4 3 2 1

Library of Congress Cataloging-in-Publication Data is available on file.

Cover and interior design by Jenny Zemanek
Cover photo credit: iStockphoto

Print ISBN: 978-1-5107-3727-3
Ebook ISBN: 978-1-5107-3728-0

Printed in the United States of America

Dedicated to my family and friends for their never-ending support and love. Special thank-yous to Michael Cohen, Erin Beck, and Jean Callum. Somewhere in heaven, I hope my father knows that his love of classic English "boardinghouse" food has been instilled in me. Every bite of a meat pie or egg tart made me think of you.

~ *Tricia*

TABLE *of* CONTENTS

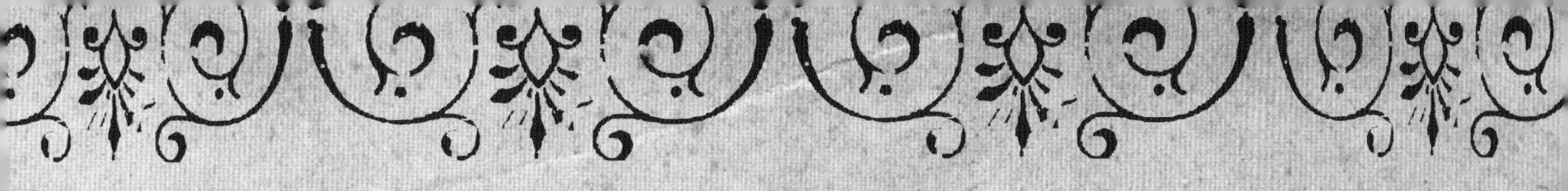

FOREWORD

You are about to embark on a journey. A delicious journey centuries in the making. A journey of wealth and a journey of poverty. A journey of historical significance and natural beauty. A journey from a modest home called Nampara to a stunning estate called Trenwith. A journey from the vibrant city of Truro to the struggling seaside towns of Cornwall. You are about to journey to the land and time of . . . *Poldark!*

Though our first glimpse of Ross Poldark is of a battered and bloodied soldier of the monarchy, it is the scene of him on his horse, Seamus, overlooking the cliffs of Cornwall that sets the stage for the beauty we are to witness throughout the BBC series and PBS's *Masterpiece* series, based on the novels by Winston Graham. Our first tug of emotions comes when Poldark enters Trenwith. A celebratory dinner is in progress, and, through his eyes, we see a table laden with food. From this point on, food will play an integral part in each and every storyline.

Yes, it is true that the stories of Poldark are indeed works of fiction. However, the time period, tribulations, and food are all very real. Whether celebratory (the parties at Trenwith), frustration (Demelza kneading or pounding dough at Nampara), aggravation (Ross Poldark eating and drinking at the Red Lion), or anticipation (the various wedding celebrations), it is food that brings all the characters and their paths together. As depicted in the series, this was a very tough time in Cornwall. Not only was the mining industry faltering, but England was also on the verge of war. It was a time of two classes of people: the rich and the poor (Ross Poldark belonging to the latter group)—and the food of the Georgian era depicted both classes perfectly.

The Unofficial Poldark Cookbook brings you the full variety of food from *Poldark's* era—from the manors and estates to the boardinghouses and shanty shacks. We will take you to wondrous breakfasts at Trenwith as well as the hearty and earthy fare of Nampara. You will learn to make breads served to miners and laborers at the Red Lion and then create luscious desserts from the most lavish parties. From the raging ocean that makes the beautiful landscape of the Cornish coast, prepare incredible seafood dishes such as "Butter Poached Cod in a Spinach Broth," "Steamed Lobster Pudding with Horseradish Sauce," and the classic boardinghouse dish "Ale Battered Fried Fish." From the gardens of Cornwall, cook up "Savory Pear, Stilton, and Honey Tart," "Butternut Cream Soup with

Port," and "Truro Turnip Gratin." From the farms, create a plethora of fabulous dishes including "Pancetta-Wrapped Pork Tenderloin," "Cider Vinegar and Honey Chicken," and the "Trenwith Ham."

True, you may never have Demelza kneading your bread or Prudie banging cast-iron pots in your kitchen, but you will find everything you need in this cookbook, whether you wish to dine like Ross Poldark or throw a party like George Warleggan and Elizabeth.

Enjoy!

The tables and kitchens of the BBC and PBS series *Poldark*, based on the novels by Winston Graham, inspired this cookbook. As you watch the series or read the novels, it will not take long for you to notice a clear class distinction between the characters—how they lived and what they ate.

We have separated this cookbook by those class distinction—"manor" and "boardinghouse."

Food at the manor was more than nutrition; it was a symbol of status and wealth. Whether a simple dinner or a grand celebration, food played an important role for the upper class during the Georgian period in England. Luxury items like brandy, canary wine, and fine ports were drank, while expensive meats, syllabubs, and glistening fruit tarts were consumed.

The manor food we have presented for you are often seen at Elizabeth and George Warleggan's table at Trenwith; Ray, Caroline, and Dr. Enys's parlor at Killewarren; and the grand and ostentatious ballroom at Tregothnan.

Cornish Rye Bread

Makes 1 loaf

INGREDIENTS

1 cup warm water
2 tsp dry yeast
1 Tbsp honey
1 cup rye flour
1 cup all-purpose flour
½ tsp salt
1 tsp caraway seeds (optional)

One of the more famous breads to come out of England is rye bread; it also happens to be one of the favorite breads on *Poldark*. This makes sense when one recalls the history of the Saxons bringing their love of rye bread—and the knowledge of how to grow rye—to Britain around 500 AD. It became a popular bread to make at home, especially in the manors of the Georgian era. Ryegrass was a plentiful crop grown on the grounds of many manors—the weather and environment of Cornwall made it easier for rye to grow than wheat.

A good rye bread goes along with any meal. Rye bread can either be made in a loaf pan or simply hand-formed into a round loaf (as was the case during the eighteenth century).

STEPS

1. In a small bowl, whisk the warm water, yeast, and honey. Set the bowl aside for 10 minutes for the yeast to proof (foam).
2. In a large bowl, whisk the rye flour, all-purpose flour, salt, and caraway seeds.
3. Stir the proofed yeast into the flour mixture until a dough is formed. Place the dough onto a floured surface and knead for 10 minutes.
4. Place the dough back into the bowl, cover, and let rise in a warm area for 2 hours.
5. Place the dough onto a floured surface and knead for 5 minutes.
6. Line the bottom of a 9x5 loaf pan with parchment paper. Form the dough into a loaf and place into the prepared loaf pan. Let the dough rise in a warm area for 90 minutes.

7. **Preheat your oven to 400 degrees. Place the bread into the oven and bake for 30–35 minutes.**
8. **Remove from the oven and let cool in the pan for 10 minutes. Then remove from the pan and cool on a wire rack.**

POTATO BREAD

Makes 1 loaf

INGREDIENTS

2 tsp dry yeast
¼ cup sugar
¾ cup warm water
6 Tbsp butter, softened
1 tsp salt
1 egg, beaten
½ cup mashed potatoes
3 cups all-purpose flour

When the scenes in *Poldark* venture into the kitchen at Nampara, you will usually see two things: Demelza or Prudie working on some dough—and a bowl of potatoes on the table. Potatoes were an important staple food of the time and were used in most dishes, including this wonderful and very light Potato Bread. It is truly wonderful bread for any dinner and was made at both the boardinghouses and the manors.

If you are the average home bread-maker, you might find this dough to be a little different. It is much moister than a usual bread dough, meaning it can get a little messy when kneading it by hand. But messy is fun! Back in the eighteenth century, this type of bread was made as a way to use up leftover mashed potatoes.

STEPS

1. In a large bowl, whisk the yeast, sugar, and warm water. Set the bowl aside for 10 minutes for the yeast to proof (foam).
2. Into the proofed yeast, whisk in the butter, salt, egg, and mashed potatoes until smooth.
3. Stir in the flour to form a dough. Place the dough onto a floured surface and knead for 10 minutes. You may need to add some extra flour while kneading, depending on the humidity of your kitchen.
4. Place the dough back into the bowl, cover, and let rise in a warm area for 2 hours.
5. Remove the dough and place onto a floured surface. Knead for 5 minutes.

6. Line the bottom of a 9x5 loaf pan with parchment paper. Form the dough into a loaf and place into the prepared loaf pan. Let the dough rise in the loaf pan for 1 hour. Don't worry if it rises over the pan.
7. Preheat your oven to 350 degrees. Place the potato bread into the oven and bake for 40–45 minutes.
8. Remove from the oven and let cool in the pan for 10 minutes. Then remove from the pan and cool on a wire rack.

BEEF HASH

Serves 4

INGREDIENTS

3 Tbsp lard

2½ cups diced potatoes (very small dice)

1 onion, peeled and minced

4 cups leftover roasted beef, minced

¾ cup beef stock

1 Tbsp tomato sauce

1 tsp ground black pepper

1 tsp salt

When you compare the two classes that made up the population of Cornwall in the era of *Poldark*, you had the rich and the poor. When it came to the food they ate, many times the ingredients were the same but the preparation was different. The poor (the villagers and, in most cases, Ross and Demelza) prepared just what was needed for the meal they would be having. The rich (like the Warleggans) would have an overabundance of food. Most of the time, leftover food from the manors like Trenwith was not wasted; it was simply made into another meal . . . like hash.

Whereas most people think of hash as being made from corned beef and coming out of a can, real hash is actually quite good and has often been made for the upper classes to go along with their eggs for a breakfast. In the Georgian era, this hash would have been made from any leftover roasted beef meat. It is quite good and rather easy to make at home.

STEPS

1. In a large skillet, melt the lard over medium heat.
2. Add the potatoes and onion, and cook for 10 minutes.
3. Stir in the minced beef, beef stock, tomato sauce, pepper, and salt. Bring to a simmer. Place a lid on the skillet and cook for 10 minutes.
4. Remove the lid and stir a few times to blend everything. Keep cooking until all the liquid has evaporated and the bottom becomes a little crusty (crisp).
5. Remove the skillet from the heat. Spoon the Trenwith Beef Hash onto a serving platter and serve.

Clotted Cream

Approximately 3 cups

Clotted cream, also called scaled and clouted cream, originated in Southwest England, but where specifically is under some debate. The counties of Cornwall and Devon both lay claim to clotted cream. Farmers, in an effort to reduce waste, would make the cream to extend the life of milk. Cookbooks as early as *The Compleat Cook* (1658) and *The Art of Cookery* (1747) published their own versions, but those recipes are not true to the Cornish style of clotted cream, which is so embedded in the region that the creamy and nutty spread is now protected. In 1998, Cornish clotted cream became a Protected Designation of Origin by the European Union. The milk must be from Cornwall, and it has to have a minimum fat content of 55 percent butterfat. The unique, slightly yellow, color in Cornish clotted cream is due to the high carotene levels in the grass.

In Cornwall, jam is spread onto the scone first, followed by a dollop of cream on top, contrary to how it is traditionally eaten in Devon where cream is layered first before jam. Any deviation from this would not be considered proper. In the words of Demelza, "T'int right, t'int fair, t'int fit, t'int proper!" In many breakfast settings at Trenwith, the Poldarks would smear Cornish cream over their jam-covered cream scone like any proper Cornish folk.

Clotted Cream makes a great topping on pies, tarts, or practically any dessert where you would add a dollop of whipped cream.

Note: Ideally, use cream that is not marked "ultra pasteurized." However, that is not always easy to find, especially in the United States.

INGREDIENTS

4 cups heavy cream

STEPS

1. Set the oven temperature to 180 degrees.
2. Pour the cream into a small oven-safe casserole dish so it comes up to a depth of 2 inches in the dish.
3. Cover the dish and place in the oven for 12 hours (yes, 12 hours). Resist touching or stirring the cream; it should be left in the oven until done.
4. Remove the dish from the oven and allow the cream to cool to room temperature. Once cooled, place in the refrigerator for 8–10 hours.
5. After the cream has chilled, carefully skim the solid cream that is floating on the top into a small bowl. The cream that remains in the casserole dish does not need to be discarded. It can be stored in a separate container and used in baking or even in your coffee (it's also delicious in rice pudding!).
6. Store the clotted cream in a covered container in the fridge. It is meant to be consumed within a few days.

Cornish Cream Scones

Makes 8 wedges

INGREDIENTS

2 cups all-purpose flour
1 Tbsp baking powder
¼ cup sugar
1 tsp salt
5 Tbsp butter, chilled and diced
1 cup heavy cream

You might not be able to find a fancy breakfast more decadent than Cornish Cream Scones. These luscious wedges of baked goodness would often be found on breakfast tables at manors, along with fresh fruit preserves and a few urns of clotted cream.

STEPS

1. Preheat your oven to 425 degrees. Line the bottom of an 8-inch round cake pan with parchment paper.
2. In a medium bowl, whisk together the flour, baking powder, sugar, and salt.
3. Add the chilled butter and, using a pastry blender (or your fingertips), cut the butter into the flour until the texture is crumbly.
4. Stir in the heavy cream until well blended.
5. Place the dough onto a floured surface and knead just until it comes together. Put the dough into the prepared cake pan and pat it down. Place into the oven and bake for 15–20 minutes.
6. Remove from the oven and turn it over onto a wire rack to cool. While still warm, cut the Cornish cream scones into wedges.

Note: These are not your typical scones. Since the only liquid used to make these scones is heavy cream, the crumb of these pastries is very delicate. Once you remove them from the oven, you want to cut them into wedges. If they cool before your cut them, they will crumble. In the *Poldark* era, these scones were formed by hand. It is much easier if you bake them in a simple round cake pan today!

CORNWALL HONEY SPICE MORNING CAKE

Makes one 8x5 loaf cake

INGREDIENTS

2 eggs, separated
½ cup sugar
½ cup vegetable oil
½ cup honey
2 Tbsp strong coffee
2 cups all-purpose flour
1¼ tsp baking powder
½ tsp baking soda
½ tsp ground cinnamon
¼ tsp ground nutmeg
¼ tsp ground cloves

Have you ever started your day with a slice of banana bread, pound cake, or any other sweet morsel to accompany your morning coffee or tea? This was one of the best ways to start a day at Trenwith, the Poldark manor house. In the show, you will often see the beloved Aunt Agatha munching away on a delicacy. One such favorite breakfast cake is the Cornwall Honey Spice Morning Cake.

Freshly harvested honey and aromatic spices were very important parts of Georgian England kitchens. Aside from creating wonderful dishes, they also sent a sweet aroma wafting through the manor. Besides being a popular morning dish at the manors, this cake would also be served to guests who visited during the afternoon, along with brandy or port.

STEPS

1. Preheat your oven to 350 degrees. Line the bottom of an 8x5 loaf pan with parchment paper.
2. In a mixer with the whisk attachment, beat the egg yolks, sugar, oil, honey, and coffee for 5 minutes. Scrape down the sides of the bowl a few times during this process.
3. In a medium bowl, whisk the flour, baking powder, baking soda, cinnamon, nutmeg, and cloves.
4. In a separate medium bowl, whisk the egg whites until stiff peaks form. Set the bowl aside.
5. Add the flour mixture to the batter and mix just until combined.

6. **Stir in half of the beaten egg whites. Then, fold in the remaining egg whites.**
7. **Spoon the batter into the prepared loaf pan. Place into the oven and bake for 65–70 minutes.**
8. **Remove from the oven and let cool in the pan 10 minutes. Then, remove from the pan and let cool on a wire rack.**

CRUMPETS

Makes 8~10

INGREDIENTS

1½ cup whole milk
1 tsp sugar
2¼ tsp yeast (1 packet)
1½ tsp salt
190 g (about 6.7 oz) bread flour
190 g (about 6.7 oz) self-rising flour
¾ cup plus 1 Tbsp tepid water
1 tsp baking soda
4" crumpet rings

Though the origin of the crumpet is a bit of a mystery, they are mentioned as early as 1382 by the English philosopher John Wycliffe in his translation of the Bible. He called them a *cromid cake*, which was more like a thin, flat cake. Early recipes of crumpets, from the late seventeenth century, used buckwheat flour and were similar to crepes. It would be nearly a hundred years later, shortly before the time Ross Poldark returned from America, that a crumpet recipe would be published in the 1769 cookbook *The Experienced English Housekeeper* by Elizabeth Raffald. By the nineteenth century, crumpets became an indispensable part of the English tea scene.

STEPS

1. Warm milk on the stovetop or in a microwave (1½ minutes). Do not boil.
2. Combine sugar and warm milk in a standing mixer bowl.
3. Sprinkle yeast evenly over the warm milk and sugar. Allow the yeast to froth, about 10 minutes.
4. Turn the mixer on low. Add salt and flours to mix. Once combined, turn mixer up to high for 3 minutes. The mixture will look smooth.
5. Turn off the mixer and remove the paddle. Cover the mixing bowl with a towel, and place in a warm area for at least 1 hour for the dough to rise.
6. Once the dough has doubled in size, mix the water and baking soda in a small mixing bowl.
7. Place the large mixing bowl with the dough back on the mixer and insert the paddle. Add the water and baking soda to the dough and mix for 1 minute until

the water is incorporated and the dough looks smooth.

8. Heat a lightly oiled (with a neutral-tasting oil) cast-iron pan or heavy skillet on medium heat.
9. Using a paper towel, rub some of the oil inside the crumpet rings. Place the rings in the pan and fill them halfway up with batter. Let the batter cook. You will know when the crumpets start to form when you see bubbles on the top. Once the bubbles begin to form, lower the heat to medium low to avoid burning on the bottom.
10. When the bottoms are nicely browned, about 4–5 minutes, gently remove the rings with tongs and flip the crumpets over. Adjust the heat back up to medium and cook the crumpets on the other side until golden brown. When done, place the crumpets on a cooling rack.
11. Before you start your next batch, wipe the inside of the rings clean as well as the pan. Repeat the cooking steps with the remaining batter.
12. Serve the crumpets with Clotted Cream (page 8), Plum and Orange Curd (page 16), or a nice helping of butter.

PLUM AND ORANGE CURD

About 2 cups

INGREDIENTS

- 4 plums
- Zest of 1 orange
- 1 packet granular gelatin
- 2/3 cup sugar
- 4 eggs, large, room temperature, and whisked
- 5½ Tbsp butter, unsalted and cut into chunks

The word *curd* appears in the fourteenth century, referring to the traditional cheese curd, a product created when milk separates into a semisolid portion from the watery whey liquid. Little Miss Muffet would be at a loss without her curds and whey! Fruit curd bears no resemblance to its dairy cousin with the same name; it is a simple mixture of fruit juice with butter, eggs, and sugar. By the nineteenth century, fruit curd became popular, especially for tea service. The Poldarks' and Warleggans' morning breakfast would have included fruit curd, along with clotted cream and scones. Our Plum and Orange Curd can also be used as a filling for tarts or macarons.

STEPS

1. Puree the plums, and strain through a fine mesh strainer. Add the orange zest and the strained plum puree to an unheated saucepan.
2. Sprinkle the gelatin over the fruit and allow it to rest for 5 minutes. Turn the heat on to medium, add the sugar, and stir.
3. When the liquid begins to boil, remove the pan from the heat. Slowly combine the eggs with the liquid, whisking briskly.
4. Put the pan back onto the stove and cook on medium heat until the thick liquid begins to boil. Remove from heat, whisk in the butter, and allow to slightly cool.
5. Add the warm liquid to a blender and mix for 1 minute.
6. Pour into a container. The mixture will be firm when cooled.

BLUEBERRY AND LEMON POSSET

Makes 4 ramekins

INGREDIENTS

2 cups heavy cream

1 cup fresh blueberries

1 cup sugar

Peel from ½ lemon (we used a vegetable peeler)

6 Tbsp fresh lemon juice

Posset, dating back to medieval times, is similar to its dessert cousin, syllabub. Historically, this English drink was made of curdled milk with wine and was a popular cold and flu remedy. In the fifteenth century, posset was made with easily accessible ingredients like milk, wine, or ale; it was seasoned with ginger—no salt, please. A century later, newly available ingredients found their way to the sweet drink recipe, such as lemon (or other citrus juices), cream, and sugar.

Verity is very skilled at making posset. She would make posset for the servants at Trenwith when they were ill and continues to make them for her Captain Blamey. Posset is mentioned in many other literary works, including Shakespeare's *Macbeth*.

We may have taken some liberties with this recipe. While whortleberries or bilberries were most likely available during the time of *Poldark*, in this recipe, we use their American cousin, blueberries, which was considered an exotic ingredient by most Europeans during the eighteenth century.

Note: If you are using frozen blueberries, they should be completely thawed

STEPS

1. Combine the cream, blueberries, sugar, and lemon peel in a medium saucepan and bring to a boil over medium heat. If the mixture begins to boil over, briefly remove from heat, stir, and then put back on the heat. Once the liquid begins to boil, cook for 10 minutes.
2. Remove the saucepan from heat and stir in the lemon juice. Let the mixture sit until slightly cooled, about 20 minutes. Strain through a fine mesh strainer into a bowl. Discard blueberries and peel. Divide the mixture evenly among ramekins or serving glasses.
3. Refrigerate, uncovered, until set, at least 3 hours. Once chilled, wrap possets in plastic wrap and refrigerate. When you are ready to serve, unwrap and sit at room temperature for 10 minutes before serving.

CANDIED ORANGE PEEL

About 2 cups

INGREDIENTS

2 oranges

4 cups water

1 Tbsp salt

4 cups sugar

Candied orange peel is a lovely sweet treat to enjoy in buns, cakes, or as a snack—today as well as during the time of *Poldark*. In the very first episode, the Poldark family is at Trenwith celebrating the engagement of Francis and Elizabeth, sitting around a dinner table that glistens with beautiful desserts like glazed fruit cakes, berries, and candied orange. Candied orange peels were consumed at both Trenwith and Nampara, crossing social lines; Demelza would most likely have used orange peel in her saffron buns or gingerbread.

Though the technique of preserving food with palm sugar has been around since antiquity, candying fruit makes a proper appearance around the fourteenth century. As the spice trade begins to open up, different foods and spices become available in Western Europe. To preserve those foods, especially fruit, for weeks, the candied technique of boiling, steeping, and dipping in sugar was used.

STEPS

1. Remove ¼" from the top and bottom of the oranges.
2. Cut the peel from each orange into sections. The white pith can remain attached, as it will mellow in the process. However, if you like, you can remove the pith from the peels.
3. In a saucepan on high heat, bring 1 cup water and the salt to boil. Once the water boils, add the peels and cook for 15 minutes. Shut the heat off, rinse, and drain the peels.
4. Bring the remaining 3 cups water and 3 cups sugar to boil in a saucepan. Stir,

and add the peels once the water begins to boil. After the water reaches boiling point once again, drop the heat down to simmer. Cook for 45 minutes and drain.

5. Place peels on a covered cookie sheet and sprinkle with the remaining 1 cup sugar, making sure each piece is covered. Leave for 30 minutes.
6. Remove the peels from the cookie sheet, add to a rack, and store in a dry space. The peels will be firm in 1–2 days.
7. Store in an airtight container. Eat as a snack, or cut it up and use in our Wheal Leisure Saffron Buns (page 88) or Figgy 'Obbin (page 100).

CHRISTMAS PLUM AND CURRANT PUDDING WITH BRANDY HARD SAUCE

Makes 1 cake

Originating during medieval times, plum pudding is a classic English dessert served during Christmas dinner. Though the original recipe called for currants and spices, it also included mutton and other meats, and it was not very sweet. Mutton cake? We think we will pass. It took a few centuries for the ingredients to develop into the flavors we enjoy today. The pudding is a moist cake with notes of warm spices and a light sweetness.

George Warleggan's desire to destroy Ross Poldark financially and personally continues in season two, when he and his Uncle Cary purchase Ross's debt just in time to bankrupt him for Christmas. Upon obtaining the debt, George states to Cary, "Do they serve plum pudding in debtors' prison?" Luckily, with Demelza's assistance, Ross was able to pay off his debt and avoid prison, and he was surely able to enjoy a delicious piece of plum pudding.

Ingredients

PUDDING:

2 cups plums (about 5 plums), pitted and pureed
1½ cup all-purpose flour
¾ tsp salt
1 tsp baking soda
1 tsp cinnamon
½ tsp nutmeg
¼ tsp cloves
1 tsp ground ginger
8 Tbsp butter, unsalted and at room temperature
½ cup sugar
½ cup brown sugar, packed
¼ cup honey
5 eggs, large
1 tsp sherry
1 tsp vanilla
1 cup currants

BRANDY HARD SAUCE:

4 Tbsp butter, unsalted and at room temperature
¾ cup powdered sugar
3 tsp brandy
Pinch of nutmeg

STEPS

1. Make the pudding. Use a blender to pulverize the plums into a puree. Set aside.
2. Preheat the oven to 350 degrees. Grease a Bundt or fluted pan.
3. In a large bowl, combine flour, salt, baking soda, cinnamon, nutmeg, cloves, and ginger. Set aside.
4. In a standing or hand mixer, whip 8 Tbsp butter until light, followed by the sugars on medium speed. Add the honey and mix well. Next, add the eggs, one at a time, while beating.
5. Once the mixture is well blended, lower the speed of the mixer and add the sherry, vanilla, and currants.
6. Now, alternate the wet and dry ingredients. While the mixer is going at medium-low speed, add a third of the dry ingredients, followed by a third of the plum. Repeat this step twice, stopping and scraping down the bowl as needed.
7. Add the mixture to the greased pan, and tightly cover the pan with aluminum foil. This is an important process because the batter will cook in two different ways—by the heat of the oven and by the steam within the pan. Cook for 55 minutes to 1 hour.
8. Slightly cool and invert onto a plate.
9. Make the brandy hard sauce. Combine 4 Tbsp butter in a mixing bowl and whip until light.
10. Turn the machine off and add powdered sugar. Slowly turn the mixer back on and add the nutmeg and brandy.
11. Add the mixture to the warm cake or serve as a side.

EARL GREY POT DE CRÈME

Serves 4

INGREDIENTS

2 cups heavy cream

½ cup whole milk

4 Earl Grey tea bags, strings removed

1 Tbsp sugar

7 large egg yolks

Dollop of Clotted Cream (page 8) (optional)

Earl Grey tea was named after Charles, the second Earl Grey, an aristocrat and highly respected politician around the time period of *Poldark*. He served in parliament from the age of twenty-two, later becoming the prime minister in 1830. While Grey enjoyed a long marriage to his wife Mary Elizabeth, he did have an illegitimate daughter with the Duchess of Devonshire, and the affair and child were the subjects of the 2008 movie *The Duchess*.

Though there are many different stories about the origin of the tea, it is said that the Earl invited a friend from China to visit him at Howick Hall. Because the friend found that the minerals in the water were not pleasant, he blended his tea with bergamot to make it more flavorful. Though Earl Grey tea is named after this colorful historical character, the Grey family never received a penny for their namesake.

Note: You can use loose tea; however, the bags make it easier to remove the tea from the crème.

STEPS

1. In a deep saucepan, add the cream, milk, and tea bags. Simmer on medium to medium-low heat for 20 minutes.
2. Remove the pan from the heat and let slightly cool. Cover, and allow it to steep in the refrigerator for 1 hour.
3. Remove the chilled cream from the refrigerator. Discard the tea bags. Place the pan back on the stovetop, and set the heat to medium. Once the cream warms, remove from heat.
4. While the cream is warming, combine the sugar and egg yolks in a mixing bowl. Slowly add the warm tea mixture into the sugar and eggs, whisking the entire time. Once fully combined, prepare a fine strainer over a bowl. Strain the mixture and discard any lumps (or cooked eggs . . . if you were a little heavy-handed with the tempering).
5. Preheat oven to 325 degrees.
6. Pour the mixture into 4 ramekins. Place the ramekins into a deep pan. Add water to the pan until the water level is halfway up the side of the ramekins. Cover the pan with aluminum foil. Place the large pan, with the ramekins, in the oven on the center rack.
7. Cook until the sides are firm and the center jiggles slightly, about 45–50 minutes. You may need to adjust the time depending on your ramekin.
8. Optional: serve with a dollop of Clotted Cream (page 8).

ELDERFLOWER SYLLABUB

4 servings, depending on ramekin size

INGREDIENTS

1½ cup whole milk

1 packet unflavored powdered gelatin

⅓ cup sugar

1½ cup heavy cream

Pinch salt

½ cup elderflower liqueur (we used St. Germain)

Word spreads quickly in Cornwall that Captain Ross Poldark has returned, and the ladies are lining up to catch the eye of the region's most eligible bachelor. In the first season, while Ross is working in his field, one such eligible maiden appears. Ruth Teague and her mother show up unexpectedly at Nampara, as Mrs. Teague attempts to show off her daughter by declaring her an accomplished rider and the maker of delicious syllabubs. Fortunately, it is Demelza who ultimately charms Ross.

Syllabub is one of the most frequently mentioned dishes in the Poldark books by Winston Graham. First appearing around the sixteenth century, the frothy, drink-ish dessert, which was wildly popular from Versailles to Buckingham, was a mixture of easily found ingredients like white wine, whipped cream, and sugar. By the eighteenth century, new versions of syllabub become available—there was whipped ("whipt"), everlasting (firm), and solid, and newly available liquors and exotic ingredients like Seville oranges were included. Here, we will make a solid, panna-cotta-like version with another popular flavor of the time, elderflower.

STEPS

1. Lightly grease your ramekins with neutral-flavored oil or spray.
2. While the heat is still off, pour milk in a saucepan on the stovetop. Sprinkle gelatin over the milk evenly. Allow the

gelatin to sit on the milk (this technique is called bloom) for 5 minutes. Do not stir.

3. Turn the heat to medium-low and allow to warm for 2 minutes before stirring. Do not allow the milk to boil; you just want to warm it up.
4. Add sugar to the milk, stir, and allow to dissolve over the heat, about 3 minutes. Remove from heat.
5. Gently whisk heavy cream, salt, and liqueur into the milk mixture.
6. Pour the mixture into the prepared ramekins, cover with plastic wrap, and cool in the refrigerator for 3 hours or more.
7. To remove the syllabub from the ramekin, dip the sides and bottom of the ramekins in warm water for 10 seconds or so. Place a small plate over the top of a ramekin, hold the two dishes together, and flip over so the syllabub will sit on the plate. Do not worry if it does not come out of the ramekin; it is still delicious.

ENGLISH WALNUT CAKE

Makes 1 cake

INGREDIENTS

½ cup butter, softened
¾ cup sugar
2 eggs, beaten
2 cups all-purpose flour
2 tsp baking powder
½ tsp salt
1 cup milk
1 cup finely chopped walnuts

As opposed to many other time periods in England, the time in which *Poldark* takes place—the Georgian era—was a pretty simple one. Whether it be in a manor or a boardinghouse, breakfast, while an important meal for the day, was very often quite plain. Eggs may have been prepared, along with smoked meat, and most of the time there was also something sweet, like this English Walnut Cake, which was usually made in a loaf form. Breakfast leftovers would often be served to guests who visited during the afternoon hours.

English walnuts are the most common of the walnut varieties. In fact, they are called *common walnuts* in Britain. How they assumed the name *English walnuts* is up for debate since their origins are somewhere near Persia (Iran). Tough English walnuts were a favorite food staple, and people did not simply throw away the shells; they were often added to the hearth to burn as they radiated more heat throughout the house.

STEPS

1. Preheat your oven to 350 degrees. Line the bottom of a 9x5 loaf pan with parchment paper.
2. In a mixer with the paddle attachment, beat the butter, sugar, and eggs for 5 minutes. Remember to scrape down the bowl a few times. In a medium bowl, whisk the flour, baking powder, and salt.

3. **Beat in half of the flour mixture, just until combined. Beat in ½ cup milk until smooth. Beat in the remaining flour mixture, just until combined. Finally, beat in the remaining ½ cup milk to form a batter.**
4. **Stir in the walnuts.**
5. **Spoon the mixture into the prepared loaf pan. Place into the oven and bake for 55–60 minutes.**
6. **Remove from the oven and let cool in the pan 10 minutes. Then, remove from the pan and let cool on a wire rack.**

HONEYCOMB CRUNCH ICE CREAM

1 container of yumminess

INGREDIENTS

ICE CREAM:

2 cups heavy cream
1 cup whole milk
1 Tbsp vanilla paste
½ cup honey
1 cup honeycomb bites (recipe below)

HONEYCOMB BITES:

1 cup sugar
6 Tbsp corn syrup
3 Tbsp honey
2½ tsp baking soda

In the eighteenth century, honey was still used widely throughout England as a sweetener for foods. Most rural farmers were self-sufficient, but some "luxury" goods were still purchased, like teas, coffee, and sugar. In the lower classes, honey was harvested by farmers, therefore there was less of an expense. Not unlike today, honey was also used for medicinal purposes, such as throat ailments.

In a dramatic turn at the end of season one, many locals in Truro and Cornwall are affected with putrid throat, a severely inflamed throat with a . . . well . . . putrid element. In one of the scenes, Demelza gives a concoction of honey, licorice, and blackcurrant to Geoffrey Charles, who is suffering. "'Twill ease the rawness," she says. When asked by Francis if he will die, Demelza responds, "Not if I can help it."

Ice cream, if you are wondering, has been made in different forms for hundreds of centuries. The icy treat appears in Europe in the thirteenth century and finally makes its way to England by the late seventeenth century, probably in the form of a sorbet.

Note: You will need an ice cream maker for this recipe.

STEPS

1. Make the ice cream. Combine cream, milk, vanilla paste, and honey in a saucepan on medium heat. Stir often. Once bubbles form around the outside, turn off the heat. You do not want this to boil.
2. Cool, cover, and chill in the refrigerator for at least 1 hour as the mixture must be cold.
3. Make the honeycomb bites. The initial process is similar to making caramel. Combine the sugar, corn syrup, and honey in a large saucepan. Cook on medium-high to high heat, without stirring. Occasionally swirl the pan to prevent the mixture from burning. Cook until sugar is completely dissolved and caramel is an amber color.
4. This next step can be tricky, so you should read this whole step first before executing. To make the honeycomb effect, quickly whisk the baking soda into the caramel. As soon as the mixtures meet, it will grow threefold. It is important to try to combine as much of the baking soda into the caramel as possible before the growth takes place, which is almost instant. Do not stir the mixture once it has grown.
5. Immediately pour the mixture onto a silicone-lined baking sheet without stirring. Let cool completely.
6. Break into bite sizes. You will need 1 cup honeycomb bites for the ice cream. Store extra honeycomb in a sealed container for a future snack.
7. Remove the chilled cream mixture from the refrigerator and add to your ice cream maker. Follow manufacturer's instructions for churning.
8. Toward the end of the churning process, add 1 cup honeycomb bites. Combine for 1 minute.
9. Transfer the ice cream to a container and store in the freezer.
10. Serve the ice cream with a sprinkle of honeycomb.

MINT LEMON CURD SHORTBREAD

Makes one 10-inch shortbread

INGREDIENTS

SHORTBREAD:

1 cup butter, softened
½ cup powdered sugar
2 cups all-purpose flour
¼ tsp salt

MINT LEMON CURD:

4 eggs
2 cups sugar
6 Tbsp all-purpose flour
1 lemon, juice and finely grated zest
1 Tbsp minced mint

When working at the mines or tending to the fishing boats, there wasn't really time to enjoy a midday snack. This was not necessarily the case if you lived at one of the manors, such as Trenwith. When visitors called or business was being attended to, oftentimes a platter of freshly made goods, both savory and sweet, was set upon the table. Though the presentation was sometimes quite elegant, the food was usually pretty simple, and one of the favorites was this Mint Lemon Curd Shortbread.

Lemons and other citrus fruits were mostly reserved for the upper classes due to their cost. Lemon curd, a type of rich lemon custard, was (and is) a favorite English dessert. Shortbread, a combination of flour, butter, and sugar, was made in most homes. We will make this dish in the common way of the time—in a cast-iron skillet.

STEPS

1. Make the shortbread. Preheat your oven to 350 degrees.
2. In a mixer with the paddle attachment, beat the butter and powdered sugar for 5 minutes. Remember to scrape down the bowl a few times.
3. Add the flour and salt, and beat just until a dough is formed.
4. Lightly oil a 10-inch cast-iron skillet. Place the dough into the skillet, and pat it down and around the rim of the skillet. Using the tines of a fork, poke holes all over the bottom of the crust. Don't worry, you can't poke too many.
5. Place in the oven and bake for 25 minutes.

6. Remove the shortbread from the oven and set aside in the skillet. Do not turn the oven off.
7. Make the mint lemon curd. In a mixer with the whisk attachment, beat the eggs and sugar for 5 minutes. Remember to scrape down the bowl a few times.
8. Add the flour, lemon juice, zest, and mint, and beat for 5 minutes. Remember to scrape down the bowl a few times.
9. Spoon the mint lemon curd into the shortbread crust. Place in the oven and bake 30 minutes.
10. Remove from the oven and let cool before serving.

ORANGE CUSTARD PUDDING

Serves 4

INGREDIENTS

2½ cups milk, divided
5 Tbsp sugar
1 orange, finely grated zest only
2 Tbsp cornstarch
2 egg yolks
¼ cup butter
½ tsp vanilla

We all have our favorite characters from *Poldark* (yes, some of us even love George Warleggan). And one thing we can all agree on is the fact that when Aunt Agatha (Caroline Blakiston) graced the screen, we were in for a true treat. Her quips and her stare brought a sense of levity to the drama, and of course her love of port and sweets made us feel better, too.

While Aunt Agatha was the Poldark matriarch, we watched her eat many dishes, and one of her favorites was a true Cornish classic—an orange custard pudding. Puddings, both savory and sweet, were a popular dish during the era, but one that contained oranges was mainly served at the manors since only the rich could afford citrus fruits.

STEPS

1. In a medium saucepan over medium heat, stir 2 cups milk, sugar, and orange zest just until the mixture comes to a simmer.
2. In a small bowl, whisk the remaining ½ cup milk with cornstarch until the cornstarch dissolves.
3. Whisk the cornstarch mixture into the hot milk mixture and cook for 2 minutes.
4. In a small bowl, whisk the egg yolks and ½ cup of the hot milk to temper.
5. Then, whisk the egg mixture into the rest of the hot milk and bring it to a simmer while whisking.
6. Remove the saucepan from the heat and whisk in the butter and vanilla until the butter melts.
7. Pour the mixture into 4 custard cups or decorative goblets.
8. Chill Orange Custard Pudding for at least 1 hour to set until ready to serve.

PORT WINE AND CHOCOLATE BONBONS

Makes 25–30

INGREDIENTS

2 cups heavy cream
½ tsp espresso powder
2 Tbsp butter, unsalted
¾ tsp salt, divided
2 Tbsp sugar
1 Tbsp vanilla paste
2½ lbs (40 oz) chocolate, divided (we used a mixture of semisweet and dark)
½ cup port
2 tsp vegetable oil
Flaky sea salt (optional)

We all cheered on the romance between the heiress Caroline and her do-gooder love, Dr. Dwight Enys. To our delight, Dwight returned to Cornwall after being held by the French, and the couple settled into their new life at Killewarren with their pug, Horace. In season three, the couple exchanged a few lines about this delicious chocolate treat, promising each other more bonbons and more kisses.

STEPS

1. In a medium saucepan, on medium heat, combine heavy cream, espresso, butter, ½ tsp salt, sugar, and vanilla paste. Do not allow the cream to boil. It will be ready once you notice bubbles form around the edges.
2. While the cream is simmering, prepare a double boiler for the next step by boiling water in a pot that is larger than the saucepan.
3. Once the cream mixture has warmed, remove the pan from the heat. Add 20 oz chocolate, along with the port, to the warmed cream as you hold the saucepan above the boiling water in the pot. The chocolate will melt into the cream. Stir often to prevent burning.
4. Once the chocolate melts, turn off the heat and allow the chocolate mixture to cool on the countertop.

5. Cover the chocolate mixture with plastic wrap and store in the refrigerator (for 4 hours) or freezer (1 hour).
6. Once the chocolate mixture is chilled, scoop out the chocolate using a melon baller and place on a lined baking sheet. If the chocolate becomes warm and tough to work with, place it back in the freezer to firm it up.
7. Store the chocolates on the baking sheet in the freezer until they firm up, about 1 hour.
8. To prepare for the next steps, place a rack over a cookie sheet.
9. Melt the remaining 20 oz chocolate, along with the remaining ¼ tsp salt and vegetable oil on the stovetop on medium heat.
10. As soon as the chocolate is melted, remove from heat and, using two forks, dip each frozen chocolate into the melted chocolate for a bath.
11. Place the dipped chocolates on the rack and sprinkle with flaky salt, if you wish. If the warm dipping mixture begins to firm in the pan, add it back onto the stovetop to melt and continue dipping.
12. After a short time, remove the chocolates from the rack (so they do not stick) and place them back on the lined cookie sheet. Pop them into the freezer to firm up, and enjoy.
13. Store in an airtight container for when you need a little pick-me-up.

Note: We always keep a finished batch in the freezer for a quick treat.

APPLE CIDER CORNISH GAMECOCK WITH ENGLISH WALNUTS

Serves 4

INGREDIENTS

1 chicken (or 2 Cornish game hens)
1 tsp salt
½ tsp ground black pepper
¼ cup melted butter
4 slices smoked bacon, chopped
1¼ cups apple cider (not apple juice)
⅓ cup brandy
1 cup heavy cream
½ cup chopped English walnuts

There seems to be a misconception about a rather famous fowl found on many dinner tables. Cornish game hens are native not to Cornwall but rather to the United States. It is Cornish *gamecocks* that belong to the Cornwall region. (The Cornish game hen is a product of breeding a Cornish gamecock and a Plymouth game hen.)

This is exactly the type of dish that would be served at the manors of the *Poldark* era for a wonderful dinner. The use of apple cider was quite popular—it would ease the gamey flavors of many of the meats and wild fowl. This dish also features one of the more popular liquors of the day, brandy (which you see imbibed often in the series). As a perfect topping to this lavish dish, we have the famed English walnuts!

STEPS

1. Preheat your oven to 400 degrees.
2. Split the chicken or hens in half by removing the backbone and ribs as they are laid flat—this is known as spatchcocking the bird. Season both sides of the bird with salt and pepper.
3. In a large skillet, heat the melted butter over medium heat. Add the chicken and brown on both sides. Remove the chicken to a platter.
4. Add the bacon to the skillet and cook for 3 minutes.

Note: Though you will not be able to find Cornish gamecocks at your local market (unless you are in Cornwall or other parts of the England), you can substitute it with chicken or Cornish game hens.

5. Remove the skillet from the heat and stir in the apple cider and brandy. Place the skillet back onto the heat and bring to a boil. Reduce the heat to a simmer and cook a few minutes until the liquid has been reduced by a third.
6. Stir in the cream. Place the chicken back into the skillet.
7. Put a cover on the skillet, place in the oven, and cook for 45 minutes.
8. Remove the skillet from the oven and place the chicken on a serving platter. Spoon the sauce over the chicken, top with walnuts, and serve.

FALMOUTH'S CHICKEN

Serves 6

The grandeur of Lord Falmouth's manor Tregothnan, a historical estate in Cornwall, conveys opulence and luxury. There would be no doubt that such a manor would have an extensive kitchen staff that was experienced in cuisine. This recipe, inspired by what is often called "white" chicken fricassee, appears in the first professional French cookbook, *Le Viandier*. This would have been a complicated dish—it is both a sauté and a stew, and it required skilled chefs to execute. We made a version that is simple and delicious, and the results will make you look like a professional chef.

INGREDIENTS

3 lb chicken thighs, boneless and trimmed
1 tsp salt
1 tsp pepper
½ cup all-purpose flour, plus 2 Tbsp
4 Tbsp unsalted butter, divided
2 Tbsp olive oil
2 sprigs fresh thyme
2 carrots, peeled and julienned
2 stalks celery, diced finely
1 onion, thinly sliced
1 cup Riesling wine
4 cups chicken stock
2 bay leaves
¼ tsp nutmeg
2 egg yolks, whisked
¼ cup heavy cream
12 oz baby spinach
2 Tbsp lemon juice
1 Tbsp tarragon

STEPS

1. Combine the chicken, salt, pepper, and ½ cup flour in a mixing bowl. Cover each piece of chicken with the flour mixture.
2. On medium-high heat, warm 2 Tbsp butter, olive oil, and thyme in a deep pan or Dutch oven.

Note: There is also a red chicken fricassee version that is made with red wine.

3. Remove the chicken from the bowl, shaking off any excess flour. Add the chicken to the hot pan, working in batches. Cook until both sides are brown and remove from the pan to set aside.
4. Lower the heat to medium, and add the carrots, celery, and onion until they begin to soften.
5. Add the remaining 2 Tbsp butter and melt. Add the remaining 2 Tbsp flour to the pan. Stir for 3 minutes until the flour soaks up all the liquid.
6. Add the wine to the pan, and stir well. Continue to cook and stir until the liquid is gone.
7. Add the chicken stock and bay leaves, stirring well to avoid lumps. Turn the heat up to medium high, and bring the liquid to a boil.
8. Add the nutmeg, stir, and return the chicken to the pan. Lower the heat to simmer and cover the pan. Cook for 20 minutes.
9. While the chicken is cooking, combine the egg yolks and cream in a small bowl. Set aside.
10. Uncover the pan and add the spinach, stir.
11. Remove a teaspoon of the liquid and slowly add it to the egg mix while stirring. Repeat that step 3 more times, raising the temperature of the eggs. Slowly drizzle the egg mixture into the pan with the chicken.
12. Finish with the lemon juice and tarragon. Salt and pepper to taste.

HERB AND CITRUS ROASTED CHICKEN

Serves 4

INGREDIENTS

- 1 whole chicken, innards removed
- 2 Tbsp melted butter
- 1 tsp minced rosemary
- 1 tsp minced thyme
- 1 tsp minced oregano
- 2 tsp salt
- 1 tsp ground black pepper
- 1 lemon, plus juice and finely grated zest

As any fan of *Poldark* is well aware, citrus fruits during this era were quite expensive and reserved for the rich—people like George Warleggan. At many of the dinner parties thrown at the various manors, you would often see roasted fowl adorning the table, surrounded by slices of various citrus fruits. These fruits were also used in the preparations of the dishes.

One of the most popular meats during this time was fowl. It could be chicken, guinea fowl, partridge, goose, duck, or, as we all witnessed in season one, pheasant (which young Jim Carter was accused of poaching). Most of the time, and especially during the holidays, the fowl was roasted with a basting of citrus juice (usually lemon or orange). Even by today's standards, this is a lovely way of preparing and presenting any type of roasted fowl.

STEPS

1. Preheat your oven to 375 degrees.
2. Wipe off any excess moisture from the chicken.
3. Place the chicken into a cast-iron skillet and rub all over with the melted butter.
4. In a small bowl, combine the rosemary, thyme, oregano, salt, pepper, and lemon zest. Sprinkle the herb mixture over the chicken.
5. Place the juiced and zested lemon into the cavity of the chicken. Spoon the lemon juice over the chicken.
6. Place the chicken in the oven and roast for 50 minutes, depending on the size of the bird. You want it to reach 160 degrees on a meat thermometer.
7. Over the course of roasting, baste the chicken with the pan juices a few times.

8. **Remove the chicken from the oven and place onto a carving board. Let the chicken rest for 10 minutes.**

9. **Spoon some of the juices over the chicken, carve, and serve.**

JUNIPER- AND ANISE-RUBBED DUCK WITH BLACKBERRY PORT SAUCE

Serves 4

INGREDIENTS

DUCK:

1 whole duck, 5.5 to 6 lb
(We used a Rohan)
2 cups boiling water
3 tsp anise seeds
24 juniper berries
½ tsp salt
¼ tsp black pepper

BLACKBERRY PORT SAUCE:

¼ cup balsamic vinegar
1 cup port wine
1 cup chicken stock
½ cup brown sugar, packed
2 tsp rosemary, minced
12 oz blackberries
4 Tbsp unsalted butter, cut into 4 pieces

Duck at the time of *Poldark* would have been wild, possessing a strong, gamey flavor. Today, we are fortunate to have wonderful purveyors from whom to purchase our duck, a product that has subtler flavors that only get better when combined with flavors like juniper and anise.

During the Georgian era, the star of this dish would have been the port. Port is one of the most popular drinks during the *Poldark* series. Port crossed all social lines—it was consumed in copious amounts in the Truro tavern The Red Lion, the Crown Inn in Bodmin, and the homes and manors like Nampara and Trenwith.

STEPS

1. Prepare the duck. Preheat the oven at 350 degrees, with a rack in the center.
2. Remove the duck from the wrapping, trim the wing tips, and remove any items in the body cavity. Thoroughly rinse the inside and outside of the duck with warm water.
3. Place the duck, breast side up, in a deep roasting pan that fits the length of the duck.

4. Using a fork, liberally prick the skin. You will want to go deep enough into the skin, but not into the flesh.
5. Pour the hot water all over the skin of the duck. This tightens the skin so that it will crisp when cooking. Allow the duck to cool for a half hour.
6. While you wait, combine the anise seeds, juniper berries, salt, and pepper in a mortar and pestle until ground down.
7. After the duck has cooled, pat the duck with paper towels, inside and out. Rub the entire bird with the spice mixture. Focus on the breast, but save some for the inside as well.
8. Place the duck in the oven. Roast for 30 minutes per pound, with the internal temperature at 165 degrees. Check on the duck often as it cooks, as the duck fat will fill up the pan. Remove the fat with a baster or simply by tilting the pan.
9. Remove the duck from the oven and let it rest for at least 10 minutes.
10. Prepare the blackberry port sauce. In a saucepan, add the balsamic vinegar and port wine. Cook on medium heat until liquids are reduced by half.
11. Add the chicken stock, and again reduce the liquids to half.
12. Add the brown sugar, rosemary and blackberries. Cook for 5 minutes.
13. Remove the pan from heat and strain the liquid through a fine mesh strainer over a bowl. Press the berries with a wooden spoon to capture all the juices.
14. Return the strained liquid to the saucepan on medium heat; discard the solids. Add one pat of butter at a time, whisking constantly until all the butter is gone.
15. Leave on the heat and set at simmer until ready.

Note: Save the fat from the duck for cooking potatoes, eggs, or French fries.

ORANGE HONEY CHICKEN

Serves 4

INGREDIENTS

1 whole chicken breast, boned and skinned (or 2 half breasts)
1 Tbsp melted butter
1 tsp minced thyme
1 tsp minced tarragon
1 tsp salt
1 tsp ground black pepper
½ cup orange juice
3 Tbsp honey

When dinners were served at the manors for big parties or special occasions, the featured dish was usually a large piece of roasted beef, pork, lamb, or fowl—and if the latter, it was usually served whole, including the head. But when dinner was served just for the family, the most popular portion of the bird was the breast, which would often be prepared with citrus.

Due to their high cost, citrus fruits were available to only the upper classes. You won't find many citrus trees lining the landscape of Cornwall and the surrounding countryside. One favorite use of citrus was in an orange glaze made with honey, which would be used with the breast of fowl or large cuts of roasted pork.

STEPS

1. Preheat your oven to 350 degrees.
2. Place the chicken breast into a skillet and rub with the melted butter.
3. Sprinkle the chicken breast with the thyme, tarragon, salt, and pepper.
4. Place in the oven and cook for 30 minutes.
5. In a small saucepan, heat the orange juice and honey until it comes to a boil. Lower the heat under the orange juice to a simmer and cook for 5 minutes.
6. Liberally brush the chicken breast with some orange glaze and cook for an additional 10 minutes or until it reaches 160 degrees on a meat thermometer.
7. Remove the chicken breast to a carving board, as you bring the orange glaze back up to a boil.
8. Slice the chicken breast, and drape with the remaining orange glaze.

PORTHCURNO CHICKEN

Serves 4

INGREDIENTS

1 whole chicken
1 lb applewood-smoked bacon, slices halved
1 orange, sliced
½ cup water
2 carrots, peeled and chopped
1 onion, peeled and thinly sliced
2 tsp salt
1 tsp ground black pepper
1 Tbsp brown sugar
½ cup chicken stock

Fans of *Poldark* have marveled at the beautiful landscape and the almost Eden-like beach where Ross can often be found chasing Demelza after one of his illogical moments. In the show, that beach is called Nampara Cove, but in reality, it is called Porthcurno and is located on the south coast of Cornwall. Its beauty, elegance, and textured layers are the inspiration for this dish.

Whereas a dish of this ilk during the time would have been made with a guinea fowl, it is much simpler and more economic to use a chicken in today's kitchen (though guinea fowl can be purchased in markets throughout Europe). It is a rather rich dish and was a favorite dinner at many manors. This recipe features applewood-smoked bacon for the ultimate flavor.

STEPS

1. Remove the innards from the chicken. Wash and dry both the outside and inside of the chicken.
2. In a medium Dutch oven over medium heat, layer half of the bacon. Place the orange slices over the bacon. Then, place the remaining bacon over the sliced oranges. Pour water over the bacon and cook for 5 minutes.
3. Add the carrots, onion, salt, pepper, and brown sugar, and cook for 3 minutes.
4. Place the chicken in the Dutch oven and pour in the chicken stock. Bring to a boil. Reduce the heat to a simmer, cover, and cook for 1 hour (basting a few times).
5. Remove the chicken to a platter and cut into serving pieces. Spoon the bacon and vegetables around the chicken, drape with sauce, and serve.

KILLEWARREN CHICKEN

Serves 6~8

The queen of Killewarren was no doubt the heiress Caroline, though we believe Horace would have thought he was the lord of the manor. This recipe was inspired by the 1390 English cooking manuscript *A Forme of Cury*, which was created by the chefs of Richard II, who was known for his grand and over-the-top feasts and celebrations. This recipe, known as *Sauce Madame*, would have used a goose, or capon, and it was said to have been served to the queen. Though you would think this to be a sweet, fruity meal, it is well balanced with a hint of autumn.

INGREDIENTS

1 cup all-purpose flour
3 tsp salt, divided
3 tsp black pepper, divided
4 lb chicken thighs
1 Tbsp olive oil
2 Tbsp butter, unsalted
2 cloves garlic, thinly sliced
1 large sweet onion, halved and thinly sliced
2 pears, quartered and thinly sliced
2 cups red seedless grapes
5 sprigs fresh thyme
3 Tbsp quince paste
1 cup Riesling wine
2 cups chicken stock
1 tsp cinnamon
1 tsp ginger
½ tsp nutmeg
½ cup fresh parsley, chopped
Bread (optional)

STEPS

1. In a shallow mixing bowl, mix flour, 2 tsp salt, and 2 tsp black pepper. Add the chicken and coat with seasoned flour.
2. In a Dutch oven on medium-high heat, add the olive oil and butter. Shake off any excess flour on the chicken and add to the pan, working in batches. Cook both sides until the skin side is crispy.
3. Remove the chicken and set aside. In the same pan, sauté the garlic and

onion. Once soft, add the pears. Gently stir after a few minutes, then add the grapes and thyme. Cook until the grapes become warm.

4. Add the quince paste to the pan, followed by the Riesling and chicken stock. Gently stir.
5. Add the cinnamon, ginger, the remaining 1 tsp salt, the remaining 1 tsp pepper, and nutmeg.
6. Stir and turn the heat to medium-high until the liquid boils. Move the dial down to medium-low, and place each piece of chicken back into the pan. Cover the pan and cook for 20 minutes.
7. After 20 minutes, remove the lid, flip the chicken over, and, using a wooden spoon, scrape up any food that is sticking to the bottom. Repeat this step two additional times. The total cooking time in the pan is 60 minutes.
8. Salt and pepper to taste. Add the fresh parsley. You can serve with bread to soak up that tasty sauce.

APPLE CIDER–BRAISED BEEF

Serves 4

INGREDIENTS

1 Tbsp lard

1 4-lb chuck roast, trimmed of excess fat

2 cups apple cider

2 onions, peeled and chopped

2 stalks celery, chopped

½ tsp ground allspice

1 tsp ground black pepper

6 whole cloves

2 potatoes, peeled and diced

4 carrots, peeled and chopped

4 parsnips, peeled and chopped

2 Tbsp butter, softened

2 Tbsp all-purpose flour

Back in the days of yore, people didn't really have the cuts of beef we have today. They simply butchered the cow, separating the tough cuts from the tender ones. The tender cuts were often roasted or grilled on an open fire, while the tougher cuts were braised. This slow cooking, especially with an acidic liquid, would naturally tenderize the beef. One of the favorite braising liquids in the Poldark era was apple cider, which was usually made at both the homes and the manors.

Since the chances are you will not be butchering your own cow to make this dish, pick up a chuck roast from the market, the typical cut of beef you would make a pot roast with. If you are not a fan of beef, you can make this with a piece of pork butt that has been trimmed of excess fat. The best way to cook this dish is in a cast-iron Dutch oven, which, interestingly enough, is how this would have been done at Trenwith!

STEPS

1. Preheat your oven to 300 degrees.
2. In a medium Dutch oven, heat the lard over medium heat. Add the chuck roast and brown on all sides.
3. In the Dutch oven, add the apple cider, onions, celery, allspice, pepper, and cloves.
4. Put a lid on the Dutch oven, place in the oven, and cook for 2½ hours, while turning the meat a few times.
5. Remove the Dutch oven and add the potatoes, carrots, and parsnips. Replace the lid, put back into the oven, and cook for 90 minutes.

6. **Remove the meat and vegetables to a serving platter. Discard the whole cloves.**
7. **Place the Dutch oven back onto the burner over medium heat. Whisk in the butter until melted. Then, whisk in the flour until the mixture thickens to a gravy.**
8. **Spoon the gravy over the meat and vegetables, and serve.**

CINNAMON AND PANCETTA-WRAPPED PORK TENDERLOIN

Serves 4–6

This dish would have been a fine meal to serve guests on a late autumn evening in Trenwith. The spices of cinnamon, cloves, and nutmeg would have complemented the port that was being served, along with other spiced, scented cakes and desserts. Aunt Agatha would have approved, considering her words in season one about her age: "Ninety-three and the appetite of a girl of twenty."

This dish is based on a recipe from the fourteenth-century French cooking manuscript *Le Menagier de Paris* for cinnamon beef. The spice trade that opened up during medieval times gave way to new flavors for the kitchens in castles, manors, and common homes. The spices were used not to mask but rather to elevate flavors.

INGREDIENTS

Spice mixture:

2 tsp cinnamon
2 tsp salt
2 tsp white pepper
1 tsp ground ginger
½ tsp ground cloves
½ tsp nutmeg

Pork:

2½–3 lb pork tenderloin
½ pound of pancetta, sliced
1 Tbsp olive oil
2 medium onions, sliced thinly
2 cloves garlic, minced
2 medium carrots, peeled and diced
1 rib celery, sliced
12 oz mushrooms (we used a mixture of portobello and oyster)
1 Tbsp rosemary, fresh and minced
3 sprigs thyme, plus extra to serve
2 bay leaves
3 cups dry Riesling wine
2 cups chicken stock

Roux:

4 Tbsp butter, unsalted
8 Tbsp all-purpose flour

STEPS

1. Make the spice mixture. Combine and mix the spices together.
2. Prepare the pork. Pat the pork dry with a paper towel. Place the pork in a shallow dish and rub the spice mix over the pork. Allow the pork to sit for 20 minutes at room temperature. You will have some mix left over; set it aside.
3. Wrap the pork with pancetta. Press any remaining spice into the pancetta.
4. In a Dutch oven or a large ovenproof pan, coat the pan with the olive oil on medium to medium-high heat. Brown all sides of the pork, even the ends. Remove the meat and set aside.
5. Preheat the oven to 375 degrees.
6. In the same pan, on medium heat, add the onions, garlic, carrots, and celery, and cook until soft.
7. Toss in the mushrooms, followed by the fresh rosemary, thyme, and bay leaves. Stir, and then add the Riesling and stock. Stir again.
8. Gently place the pork into the pan, cover, and put into the oven for 80–90 minutes. The meat should have an internal temperature of 145 degrees.
9. Remove the pan from the oven, remove the pork, and tent in foil.
10. Place the *very* hot pan onto the stovetop over medium heat. Cook down the juices for 15 minutes. Remove the bay leaves.
11. Make the roux in a separate pan. Melt the butter, and when it begins to bubble, sprinkle the flour into the butter and stir vigorously. Remove a cup of juices from the large pan and slowly mix it into the roux. Pour the roux into the large pan, and stir.
12. Sprinkle with fresh thyme. Cut the pork and serve with the gravy.

MANOR HAM

Serves 6~8

INGREDIENTS

10–13 lb ham, on the bone
1 cup apricot and orange preserves
½ cup honey
1 tsp fresh thyme
1 tsp ground ginger
¼ tsp salt
1 bottle hard cider (12 oz)
4 Tbsp butter, unsalted

It is hard not to want to have dinner at Trenwith, considering every scene set in that manor features perfectly crafted meals and desserts. The food glistens with glazed meats and cakes, an abundance of vibrant fruit, and the ever-full glass of port sparkling under candlelight. This ham would have been one of those glistening delights, as seen in season one. As the ham bakes, the apricot and orange preserves, along with the honey, create a glazed top that creates the perfect balance between sweet and salty.

STEPS

1. Place the ham on a cutting board. Using a sharp knife, score the fat in a diamond pattern, cutting all the way through to the meat. Put the ham in a large roasting pan.
2. In a mixing bowl, combine the apricot and orange preserves, honey, thyme, ginger, and salt. Stir. Spread the mixture over the fat of the ham.
3. Pour the cider over the ham. Cover the pan and marinate the ham in the refrigerator for several hours or overnight.
4. Preheat the oven to 325 degrees. Remove the ham from the refrigerator and allow it to rest for 20 minutes. Spoon the marinade from the pan over the ham.

Note: If you cannot find this mixed preserve, you can also use marmalade.

5. **Place the roasting pan with the ham in the oven and cook for 12–15 minutes per pound, between 2 to 2½ hours. The meat should have an internal temperature of 145 degrees. After 1 hour of cooking, baste the ham every so often so it glistens and does not dry out.**
6. **Remove the ham from the oven, cover, and set aside to rest for 1 hour.**
7. **Do not throw out the pan juices. Place the roasting pan on the stovetop on medium heat and boil down for 10 minutes. Add the butter, stir, and continue to cook for another 5 minutes.**
8. **Before serving, pour the juices over the ham.**

SPICED APPLE-PLUGGED LEG OF LAMB

Serves 4

INGREDIENTS

1 leg of lamb (5 lb)
2 Tbsp melted butter
1 Tbsp minced thyme
1 Tbsp minced sage
1 Tbsp minced tarragon
1 Tbsp salt
1 tsp ground black pepper
⅓ cup sugar
⅓ cup apple cider vinegar
3 Tbsp water
3 Tbsp honey
¼ tsp ground cinnamon
⅛ tsp ground cloves
2 apples; peeled, cored, and cut into 8 wedges

The preferred method of cooking meat was roasting. In some homes, this meant roasting over an open hearth, and in the manors, it meant roasting in a brick or stone oven. Whether it was fowl, beef (rather uncommon), goat, or lamb, a dinner featuring a roast was indeed a celebration.

Spiced Apple Plugged Leg of Lamb was a dinner that would have been served on a special occasion, such as Christmas, along with pheasant, goose, and, depending on the manor, a small suckling pig. Spices such as cinnamon and cloves were pretty much reserved for the upper classes due to their cost.

Note: While a bone-in leg of lamb was always used to make this dish during Georgian times, you can use a boneless leg of lamb, which most markets have in stock year-round.

STEPS

1. Preheat your oven to 325 degrees.
2. Place the leg of lamb on roasting rack in a roasting pan. Rub the lamb with the melted butter and sprinkle over the thyme, sage, tarragon, salt, and pepper.
3. Put the leg of lamb into the oven and roast for 2½ hours (the time will be shorter if using a boneless leg of lamb).
4. In a large skillet over medium heat, combine the sugar, apple cider vinegar, water, honey, cinnamon, and cloves, and bring to a boil.
5. Add the apples and cook for 7 minutes, while stirring.
6. Remove the leg of lamb from the oven. Using a sharp paring knife, make deep slits in the leg of lamb and plug each with a wedge of apple. Spoon the syrup over the leg of lamb.
7. Place the leg of lamb back into the oven and roast for 20 more minutes.
8. Remove from the oven and place on a carving board to rest for 10 minutes. Carve the leg of lamb and serve with the apples.

VEAL AND MUSHROOM COLLOPS WITH MADEIRA SAUCE

Serves 4

A *collop*, which might have originated from the French word *escalope*, is an old term for slices of meat, often served cold. In the seventeenth century, the word *collop* becomes associated with bacon, and the philosopher and diplomat Kenelm Digby speaks about collops of pure bacon along with eggs as a fine breakfast. In many of the eighteenth century cookbooks published during the Georgian era, recipes use the word *collops*, which suggests that it began to broaden to include warm dishes. This recipe is inspired by an early nineteenth-century recipe for Scotch collops that cooked slices of veal in egg and nutmeg.

INGREDIENTS

- ¾ lb veal cutlets
- 1 cup all-purpose flour
- ½ tsp ground nutmeg, plus ⅛ teaspoon for the sauce
- ¼ tsp salt
- ¼ tsp pepper
- 1 egg, large and beaten
- At least 1 Tbsp unsalted butter
- 1 small sweet onion, thinly sliced.
- 1 clove garlic, minced
- 1 cup mushrooms, chopped (we used oyster mushrooms)
- ½ cup Madeira wine
- ½ cup chicken stock
- ⅛ teaspoon cinnamon
- 1 Tbsp heavy cream
- Flat leaf parsley, minced (optional)

STEPS

1. Place veal cutlets between two pieces of wax paper, and lightly pound until ¼-inch thick.
2. Mix flour, ½ tsp nutmeg, salt, and pepper in a shallow dish. In a separate shallow dish, add beaten egg.
3. Pat the veal dry with paper towels. Dunk the veal into the egg, followed by the flour mixture, and set aside. Repeat until all pieces are covered.
4. In a deep sauté pan, add 1 Tbsp butter and melt on medium-high heat. Cook

veal for 2 minutes on each side. Add additional pats of butter as needed; you do not want the veal to burn. If your veal is thicker or thinner, adjust your cooking time. Place cooked veal on a plate and set aside.

5. In the same sauté pan, add onions and garlic. Cook until onion starts to become tender, then add mushrooms.
6. Once mushrooms are soft, add Madeira wine and scrape up the bits on the bottom of the pan, while stirring. Add chicken stock, cinnamon, and the remaining ⅛ tsp nutmeg.
7. Once the sauce fully incorporates all the ingredients, add the cream, and salt and pepper to taste. Return the veal to the pan, spooning the sauce and vegetables over the veal.
8. Finish with a sprinkle of parsley.

LEMON AND TARRAGON WHITEFISH

Serves 4

INGREDIENTS

- 2 Tbsp butter, divided
- 1 lb whitefish, cut into 4 portions
- ⅓ cup dry white wine
- 2 tsp lemon juice
- 2 scallions, minced
- 1 tsp minced tarragon
- ¼ tsp finely grated lemon zest
- ½ tsp salt
- ¼ tsp ground black pepper

When dinner was served at a party in one of the Cornwall manors, the visual of the food was oftentimes just as important as the food itself. Each dish was plated in the kitchen by the staff and brought out to the table individually. This was done for two reasons: first, the owner of the manor could show off his staff, and second, the dishes would be brought to the table fresh and hot.

A dish such as this Lemon and Tarragon Whitefish was commonplace for manor dinner parties. It featured the whitefish that was caught that day, and its simple recipe made it possible for the kitchen staff to prepare other more time-consuming dishes. This is one of the more elegant dishes prepared from the era as it features a white wine (use a French wine for authenticity) and a light lemon fragrance.

STEPS

1. Melt 1 Tbsp butter in a large skillet over medium heat.
2. Add the whitefish and cook about 7 minutes per side (depending on the variety and thickness of the fish). Remove the fish to a platter and keep warm.
3. Into the skillet, whisk the white wine, lemon juice, scallions, and tarragon, and let cook for 2 minutes.
4. Remove the skillet from the heat and whisk in the remaining 1 Tbsp butter, lemon zest, salt, and pepper.
5. Spoon the sauce over the fish and serve.

SAINT GEORGE'S WHITEFISH AND SPARROW GRASS

Serves 4

INGREDIENTS

- 1 lb whitefish, cut into 4 portions
- ½ tsp salt
- ¼ tsp ground black pepper
- 1 onion, peeled and minced
- 1 carrot, peeled and minced
- ¼ cup chicken stock
- 2 cups chopped asparagus

Since history in the United Kingdom has been recorded, sparrow grass has always been one of the most popular vegetables. Though its growing season is very short, only from April until the beginning of June, it was, and still is, a great ingredient for festivities. It is usually referred to in conjunction with Saint George's Day (the Patron Saint of England) on April 23, when the first harvest would usually begin. It should be noted that the name *sparrow grass* was looked down upon by the upper classes of the day, who instead decided to call it . . . asparagus!

Asparagus was a very popular crop in Cornwall and its surrounding areas. In fact, one of the largest growers of asparagus today is located in Truro. This dish, which was a popular meal at manors during the short growing season, features two of the *Poldark* era's most popular ingredients—whitefish and asparagus.

STEPS

1. Place the whitefish into a medium skillet. Add the salt and pepper.
2. Place the onion and carrots over the fish. Pour chicken stock over the ingredients. Top with the asparagus.
3. Place the lid on the skillet or cover with foil. Put into the oven and bake for 20 minutes.
4. Remove from the oven and serve.

PUFFED WHITEFISH

Serves 4

INGREDIENTS

- 1 lb whitefish, cut into 4 sections
- ½ tsp salt
- ¼ tsp ground black pepper
- 1 egg white
- ¼ cup mayonnaise
- ½ tsp minced thyme

When you look back on the history of cooking, ingenuity is always the main ingredient. Among the ingredients in this dish is mayonnaise, and you might think mayonnaise wasn't available during the *Poldark* era, but it was, albeit not the type you buy at the market today. They made their own (which is simple to do)—the main difference is they added a little more egg white to the emulsification. And we're going to do that with this recipe!

Here, you can use any variety of whitefish. Fish of the fleshy variety is recommended as this dish will be baked and it needs to hold together during that process. Since a dish like this took constant watching (remember, they baked over an open flame), it was usually only served at manors with a kitchen staff. This dish gets its name because the mayonnaise mixture covering the fish will puff up during the baking process.

STEPS

1. Preheat your oven to 425 degrees.
2. Place the fish into a skillet or casserole pan and sprinkle with salt and pepper.
3. In a small bowl, whisk the egg white until stiff peaks form.
4. In another small bowl, stir the mayonnaise and thyme.
5. Fold the beaten egg white into the mayonnaise mixture. Spoon the mixture over the whitefish fillets.
6. Place into the oven and bake for 15–20 minutes (depending on the variety of fish used).
7. Remove from the oven and serve.

STEAMED BASS WITH PURÉED LEEKS AND HERBS

Serves 4

INGREDIENTS

5 cups water, divided
1 leek; tender white portion only, thinly sliced
½ cup fish stock
1 Tbsp cider vinegar
1 Tbsp butter
2 Tbsp minced dill
1 tsp minced thyme
1 lb sea bass, in ¼-lb portions
1 tsp salt
½ tsp ground black pepper

Remember: the era of *Poldark* was one of no electricity or gas power. When it came time for cooking, the hearths had to be fired up (notice how you always see characters on the show cutting wood). Most of the time, there was a fire going, and over those flames was a metal rod upon which pots were hung. One of those pots always contained water, which explains why steaming was a popular way to prepare food.

When one thinks of Cornwall, wonderful seafood dishes are brought to mind. There are over four hundred miles of coastline, with the Atlantic Ocean covering the north coast and the English Channel covering the south coast. No matter the era, seafood is a staple of any Cornish kitchen, and this Steamed Bass with Puréed Leeks and Herbs is a Cornish classic!

Steps

1. In a medium saucepan, bring 2 cups water to a boil. Add the leek, cover, and cook for 5 minutes.
2. With a slotted spoon, remove the leek and place in a food processor with the fish stock, vinegar, butter, dill, and thyme. Purée the mixture. Spoon the purée into a small bowl, and set aside.
3. In a steamer, bring the remaining 3 cups water to a boil.
4. Season the sea bass with salt and pepper. Place the sea bass into the basket of the steamer, cover, and steam for 10 minutes (depending on the thickness off the fish).
5. Place the steamed bass onto serving plates, drizzle with some sauce, and serve.

STEAMED LOBSTER PUDDING WITH HORSERADISH SAUCE

Serves 4

There are two main lifestyles in *Poldark*—you have the simplicity of the miners, fishermen, and Ross and Demelza; and then you have the extravagance of George Warleggen and Elizabeth. Whereas the typical resident of Cornwall might enjoy a rich and hearty chowder from a day's catch, at the manors, they would partake of something a little more chic—such as this Steamed Lobster Pudding with Horseradish Sauce.

Though the dish may seem quite elegant (and it is), it is very simple to make. Most of the dishes in the era, no matter the class style they were prepared in, were simple.

INGREDIENTS

¼ cup butter
1 Tbsp Worcestershire sauce
2 lobster tails, shells removed and meat chopped
1 parsnip, peeled and julienned
1 leek; tender white portion only, and thinly sliced
½ cup dried bread crumbs
2 eggs, beaten
1 Tbsp heavy cream
¼ lb shaved cured or smoked ham
¼ cup sour cream
1 Tbsp horseradish

STEPS

1. In a medium skillet over medium heat, melt the butter into the Worcestershire sauce. Add the lobster and cook for 3 minutes. Remove the lobster meat with a slotted spoon and set aside.
2. Into the skillet, add the parsnip and leek and cook for 5 minutes. Remove the pan from the heat and set aside.
3. In a small bowl, combine the bread crumbs, eggs, and heavy cream.
4. Lightly oil the bottoms and sides of 4 large ramekins or custard cups. Line the bottoms and sides with shaved ham. Make sure it overlaps as you will be folding it over to encase the custard.
5. Into the ham-lined ramekins, layer the vegetable mixture and lobster meat, finishing with a top layer of lobster. Pack it down tightly with your hands.

6. Place the bread crumb mixture over the top layer of lobster. Fold the overlapping shaved ham over the pudding and set aside 10 minutes to rest.
7. Fill a steamer with 4 cups of water and bring to a boil. Place the ramekins into the steamer basket. Lower the heat to a simmer, cover the pot, and steam 40 minutes. Remember to check the water level during this time and add more if needed.
8. In a small bowl, whisk the sour cream and horseradish.
9. Remove the lobster puddings from the steamer and let cool for 10 minutes.
10. Run a knife around the perimeter of the ramekins and invert the pudding onto serving plates. Top with a dollop of horseradish cream and serve.

Note: If you don't have a steamer, you can put the ramekins in a deep skillet. Fill the skillet halfway up the sides of the ramekins with water, place a lid on the skillet, and simmer until done.

BARLEY SOUP

Serves 4

INGREDIENTS

2 Tbsp butter
1 onion, peeled and minced
4 scallions, minced
2 carrots, peeled and chopped
2 stalks celery, chopped
1 cup chopped smoked ham
½ cup barley
1 Tbsp all-purpose flour
4 cups chicken stock
2 egg yolks
⅓ cup heavy cream

The landscape and climate of Cornwall and its surrounding areas make it one of the best places to grow the cereal grain known as barley. Historically, barley was one of the first grains to be cultivated over ten thousand years ago. During the *Poldark* era, most of the manors and homesteads grew the grain, and you can see people harvesting it in a few episodes. When processed, barley was used in baked products; and, as a whole grain, it makes for a wonderful addition to many soups.

When you live without power, as they did during the eighteenth century, you have to preserve food naturally. The two most common ways were with salt and by smoking meat. This is why you will often see smoked meats used in the dishes of the time. This soup features smoked ham; you can also use smoked pork belly (bacon).

STEPS

1. In a medium saucepan, melt the butter over medium heat.
2. Add the onion, scallions, carrot, and celery, and cook for 5 minutes.
3. Add the ham and barley, and cook for 3 minutes.
4. In a medium bowl, whisk the flour and chicken stock. Stir the chicken stock into the saucepan and bring to a boil. Reduce the heat to a simmer and cook for 90 minutes.
5. In a small bowl, whisk the egg yolks and cream. Slowly stir the cream mixture into the soup and cook for 10 minutes.
6. Ladle into bowls and serve.

BROCCOLI AND STILTON CREAM SOUP

Serves 4

INGREDIENTS

2 tsp vegetable oil
1 onion, peeled and minced
1 stalk celery, minced
1 leek; tender white part only, minced
1 Tbsp butter
4 cups chicken stock
1 head broccoli, chopped
⅔ cups Stilton cheese, crumbled

Whether it be a day working in the mines, pulling in nets of fish, or going over your fortunes in the comfort of your manor, nothing warms the body and soul quite like a steaming bowl of freshly made soup. While we would likely make this soup on a stovetop, in the *Poldark* era, this soup simmered in an open hearth, warming up the entire kitchen.

Stilton cheese is an English blue cheese that originated in Stilton, England, now known as Cambridgeshire. As it melts into the soup, you'll get a beautiful, creamy texture, hence the name of this soup even though no cream is added.

STEPS

1. In a medium saucepan, heat the oil over medium heat. Add the onion and cook for 5 minutes.
2. Stir in the celery, leek, and butter, and cook for 5 minutes.
3. Add the chicken stock and broccoli and bring to a boil. Reduce the heat to a simmer and cook for 10 minutes.
4. Place the soup into a food processor in batches and puree. Pour the soup back into the pan and heat just until it comes to a simmer.
5. Remove the soup from the heat and stir in the Stilton cheese.
6. Ladle into bowls and serve.

Note: You can use any other blue cheese if you can't find Stilton.

BUTTERNUT CREAM SOUP WITH PORT

Serves 4

During lavish dinner parties at manors, a multitude of courses were delivered to the table. Among these courses, and before the entree, was always a soup. In most cases, it was a rich cream soup that featured produce from the garden, such as this Butternut Cream Soup with Port. Poldark's favorite wine, port, is used here to bring out the soup's natural flavors with its sweet profile.

INGREDIENTS

¼ cup butter
3 cups diced butternut squash
2 scallions, minced
1 tsp ground cinnamon
1 cup chicken stock
1 cup heavy cream (half-and-half can be substituted)
½ cup port

STEPS

1. In a medium saucepan, melt the butter over medium heat.
2. Add the butternut squash, scallions, and cinnamon, and cook for 10 minutes.
3. Stir in the chicken stock and bring to a boil. Reduce the heat to a simmer and cook for 20 minutes, or until the butternut squash is fork tender.
4. Spoon the ingredients into a food processor and puree.
5. Pour the puree back into the saucepan over medium heat. Stir in the cream and bring to a simmer.
6. Remove the saucepan from the heat, stir in the port, and serve.

Note: Once Britain went to war with France from 1793 to 1794 (which is when Poldark leaves Cornwall to save Dr. Enys in France in season three), they no longer drank port as most of it was imported from France.

CORNISH CREAM OF CHICKEN SOUP

Serves 4

Though this soup was often made with whatever fresh fowl was in season, today it is made almost solely using chicken. If, perchance, you have recently hunted some pheasant or other such fowl, you can use that, but the cooking time will be different depending on the bird.

Cornish Cream of Chicken Soup is a very thick and rich soup. As a main course, it would usually be served over cooked grains; and if it was served as part of a multicourse dinner, it would be dished up in shallow soup plates. Unlike many soups of the era, this soup features only meat, as the vegetables cooked with it are eventually sieved out.

INGREDIENTS

1 whole chicken, innards and excess fat removed
6 cups water
4 stalks celery, chopped
1 onion, unpeeled and quartered
4 sprigs thyme
4 whole peppercorn
4 whole juniper berries
3 Tbsp all-purpose flour
1 cup heavy cream, divided
1 cup milk
3 Tbsp butter
1 tsp salt

STEPS

1. In a medium or large Dutch oven over high heat, add the whole chicken and the water, celery, onion, thyme, peppercorns, and juniper berries, and bring to a boil.
2. Reduce the heat to a simmer, cover, and cook for 2 hours.
3. Remove the chicken from the Dutch oven and set aside. Strain the cooking liquid through a fine sieve and discard the solids. Pour the stock back into the Dutch oven.
4. Remove the meat from the chicken. Discard the bones, fat, and skin.

5. **In a small bowl, whisk the flour and ½ cup heavy cream. Whisk this mixture into the soup. Then, whisk the remaining ½ cup heavy cream, milk, butter, and salt into the soup and bring to a boil.**
6. **Reduce the heat to a simmer and stir in the chicken meat. Cook for 5 minutes.**
7. **Ladle into bowls and serve.**

DEEP CREAM FISH CHOWDER

Serves 4

INGREDIENTS

2 Tbsp butter
1 onion, peeled and minced
3 cups heavy cream
1 cup milk
1 tsp minced thyme
¼ lb smoked bacon, diced
2 potatoes, peeled and diced
1½ lb whitefish, cubed
1 tsp salt
½ tsp ground black pepper
Crusty bread (optional)

When you live in one of the most beautiful coastal areas in the world, your diet contains a lot of seafood. It may be fried, boiled, or put into a pie—or, in the case of this dish, featured in one of the most richly delicious chowders you will ever taste.

In addition to seafood, Cornwall and its surrounding areas were (and still are today) world renowned for their dairy products, especially their creams—Devonshire Cream and Cornwall Cream, two of the most prized in the world. This Deep Cream Fish Chowder may be a dieter's nightmare, but it is also a fish lover's dream come true. As with all dishes from the *Poldark* era, use whitefish or the next two best options, cod or halibut.

STEPS

1. In a medium Dutch oven, melt the butter over medium heat.
2. Add the onion and cook for 5 minutes.
3. Stir in the heavy cream, milk, and thyme, and bring to a boil. Reduce the heat to a simmer and cook 15 minutes.
4. In a medium skillet over medium heat, add the bacon and cook until crisp. Remove the bacon with a slotted spoon and set aside.
5. Into the chowder, add the potatoes and cook for 10 minutes or until fork tender.
6. Stir in the fish, salt, pepper, and bacon, and cook for 15 minutes.
7. Ladle into bowls and serve with crusty bread if you like.

PIPPINS AND CABBAGE

Serves 4

INGREDIENTS

- 2 Tbsp butter
- 1 head red cabbage, core removed and leaves shredded
- 3 Pippin apples, cored, peeled and thinly sliced
- 3 Tbsp honey
- ¼ cup port wine
- ¼ cup chicken stock
- 1 tsp salt

Though you do not often see fresh produce served at the dinners on *Poldark*, they were a very important aspect of the diet of the time. In some of the party scenes at the manors, bowls of fruit are placed on the table as colorful decoration. Produce played a significant role in the economy of Cornwall, and two of the most popular kinds of produce were cabbages and apples.

Pippins and Cabbage has been a popular dish for centuries in areas where cabbage is abundant. What are "pippins?" They are a variety of apple—almost a cross between a green and red apple. Their flavor marries wonderfully with cabbage, and when accompanying a main course featuring roasted fowl or pork, you have the makings of a very delicious and very Georgian-era dinner!

STEPS

1. In a large skillet, melt the butter over medium heat.
2. Add the cabbage and cook for 7 minutes.
3. Stir in the apples, honey, port, chicken stock, and salt. Bring to a simmer and cook for 10 minutes.
4. Remove from the heat and let cool slightly before serving.

SAVORY PEAR TART WITH STILTON AND HONEY

Serves 4

Classic English ingredients make up this recipe. Stilton cheese has been produced in England since at least the early part of the eighteenth century, and honey was historically used as a sweetener. On the Trenwith table, pears make an appearance, often poached or on sweets. We took these three ingredients and made them into a sweet and savory tart.

INGREDIENTS

Savory Piecrust Dough (page 126)
2 Tbsp butter, unsalted
1 large sweet onion, thinly sliced
2 cloves garlic, minced
⅛ tsp salt
4 pears, thinly sliced
4 oz Stilton cheese, crumbled
1 tsp fresh thyme
1 Tbsp honey, plus more to taste

STEPS

1. Roll out the dough on a lightly floured surface until it easily fits the size of the pan you're using, with some overlap, and is approximately ¼ inch thick. We used a 13¾ × 4½ tart pan with a removable bottom. Using your fingers, press the dough into the sides and corners of the pan. Using a rolling pin, roll over the dough at the top of the pan for an even edge. Chill the dough in the pan for 30 minutes.
2. Preheat oven to 350 degrees. Remove the pan from the refrigerator, and immediately place in the oven for 20 minutes to bake the crust.
3. Melt butter in a sauté pan on medium heat. Add onion, garlic, and salt. Once the onion is soft, remove the pan with the dough from the stove and let cool.
4. Increase the oven temperature to 400 degrees.

5. Layer the tart with the onions, followed by the Stilton. Layer the pears evenly over the cheese, followed by the thyme and honey.
6. Bake the tart in the oven for 12–15 minutes, removing once the pears become golden.
7. Add another swirl of honey, if so desired (we did!), and slightly cool before serving.

Boardinghouse

Food at the boardinghouses and in the lower classes consisted of hearty meals made with inexpensive ingredients. Dishes were basic and simple but still delicious. Though Ross and Demelza had a larger home at Nampara, they ate more like a boardinghouse then a manor. Perhaps that was a result of Demelza's humble childhood or Ross's assimilation to the worker culture at the mine. Boardinghouses like the Red Lion served mead, ale, and cider, along with hearty stews, bread, and meat pies.

The food the lower class ate depended on what was available, and many times, very little was. During the time of *Poldark*, the poor outnumbered the wealthy in great numbers and food was a necessity, not a luxury. Poor harvests, expenses from war, and lack of work greatly affected this population.

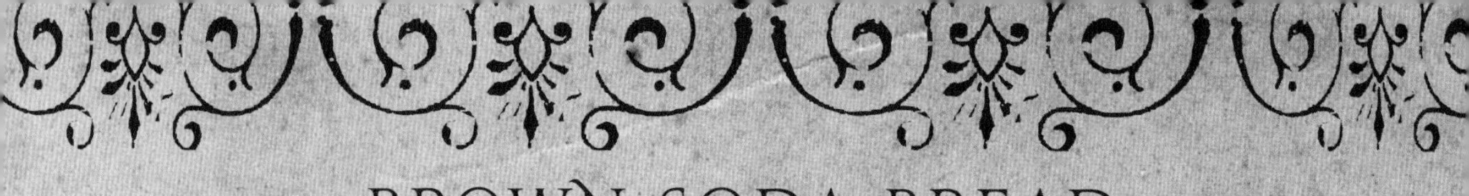

BROWN SODA BREAD

Makes 1 round loaf

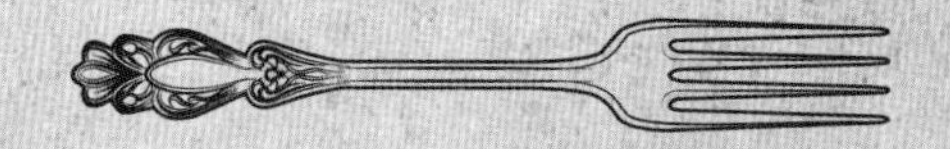

INGREDIENTS

- 2¼ cups whole-wheat flour
- 2¼ cups all-purpose flour
- 1 tsp salt
- 1½ tsp baking soda
- 2 cups buttermilk

What is that flat, round loaf of bread that Ross Poldark often eats at the kitchen table in Nampara? It is brown soda bread, a classic bread from the era, which, according to lore, may have originated in Ireland (which is interesting since Aiden Turner is Irish). Since it doesn't require yeast, it was popular to make at the time when you needed a bread on the table rather quickly.

Back in the day, brown soda bread was made using sour milk. No, nothing went to waste in an eighteenth-century kitchen. For today's version, we use a buttermilk. The difference between a regular soda bread and a brown soda bread is the flour—the latter uses a combination of whole-wheat flour and the typical white flour. Today, of course, we use "all-purpose flour."

STEPS

1. Preheat your oven to 400 degrees. Line a baking sheet with parchment paper or a silicone sheet.
2. In a large bowl, whisk the wheat flour, all-purpose flour, salt, and baking soda.
3. Stir in the buttermilk to form a dough.
4. Place the dough onto a floured surface and knead for 5 minutes. Form the dough into a ball and flatten with your hands until about 2 inches thick.
5. Place the dough onto the prepared baking sheet and, with a sharp paring knife, make a shallow "X" in the middle of the dough.
6. Place into the oven and bake for 25–30 minutes.
7. Remove from the oven and let cool on a wire rack.

HERB CURD CHEESE BREAD

MAKES 1 LOAF

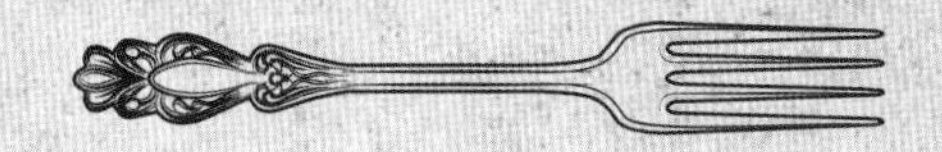

INGREDIENTS

- 1 Tbsp honey
- 2½ tsp dry yeast
- ½ cup warm water
- 2½ cups all-purpose flour
- 1 cup cottage cheese (small curd), drained
- 1 egg, beaten
- 2 scallions, minced
- 1 Tbsp sugar
- 1 tsp salt
- 1 Tbsp minced basil
- 1 Tbsp minced rosemary
- 2 Tbsp melted butter

The homesteads of the villagers in Cornwall provided the locals with most of their food, from produce to meat and even dairy products. Many of the homesteads had goats or a cow or two, from which they got their milk. And as the adage goes, "Where there is milk, there will be cheese." Whether it be from a cow or a goat, the art of making cheese was practiced in most homes. One of the more popular cheeses to make at home was a curd cheese or, as it is better known today, a cottage cheese. In fact, the name *cottage cheese* came about because it was made at home in a cottage.

This particular bread features curd cheese and the usual herbs grown in the gardens.

STEPS

1. In a small bowl, whisk the honey, yeast, and water. Set the bowl aside for 10 minutes to proof (foam).
2. In a large bowl, stir the flour, cottage cheese, egg, scallions, sugar, salt, basil, rosemary, and the proofed yeast. You will have more of a batter than a dough.
3. Cover the bowl and let rise for 2 hours in a warm area.
4. Stir the dough down. It will still be too wet to knead. Line the bottom of a 9x5 loaf pan with parchment paper, and spoon the dough into the pan. Let rest for 30 minutes.
5. Preheat your oven to 350 degrees. Place the bread into the oven and bake for 10 minutes.
6. Remove the bread from the oven and brush the top with the melted butter. Place the bread back into the oven and bake for 35–40 minutes.
7. Remove the bread from the oven and let cool in the pan for 10 minutes. Then, remove from the pan and let cool on a wire rack.

RED LION CHOWDER BREAD

Makes 8 pieces

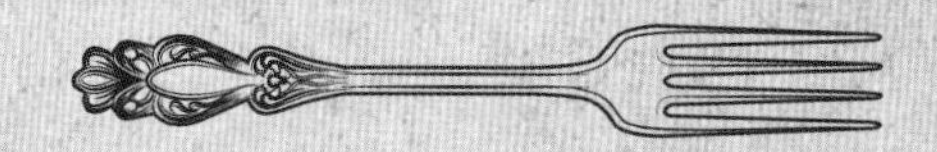

INGREDIENTS

4 cups all-purpose flour
¼ cup sugar
2 tsp salt
3 Tbsp lard
2½ tsp dry yeast
1¾ cups water

Imagine, if you will, walking along the shopping area of Cornwall in 1790 and venturing into the Red Lion for a pint of ale. Aside from the possibility of running into Ross Poldark, Francis Poldark, or Doctor Dwight Enys, you would also enjoy a piping hot bowl of fresh seafood chowder made from the day's catch, served alongside a bread made especially for soaking up all that wonderful broth. With its delicate crust and almost angelic inner texture, these breads (rolls by today's measure) were torn apart and dipped into the soup. Though created to complement chowder, Red Lion Chowder Bread is an outstanding bread for any occasion. This type of bread was made solely at the boardinghouses and inns.

STEPS

1. In a large bowl, combine all the ingredients to form a dough. There is no need to proof the yeast.
2. Place the dough onto a floured surface and knead for 10 minutes. Place the dough back into the bowl, cover, and let rise for 1 hour in a warm area.
3. Repeat step 2. Place the dough onto a floured surface but knead for 5 minutes. Place the dough back into the bowl, cover, and let rise for 1 hour in a warm area.
4. Divide the dough into 8 portions and form each into a ball. Place the portions of dough onto the prepared sheet and let rise for 30 minutes.
5. Preheat your oven to 450 degrees. Place into the oven and bake for 15–20 minutes.
6. Remove from the oven and let cool on a wire rack.

Note: This dough is a little stickier than most bread doughs, which is what gives the bread (rolls) an incredible texture

WHEAL LEISURE SAFFRON BUNS

MAKES ABOUT 10 BUNS

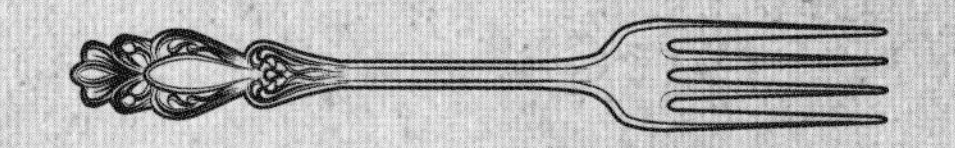

INGREDIENTS

½ tsp saffron threads
2 Tbsp hot water
1 Tbsp yeast
1½ Tbsp sugar
5 Tbsp warm water
1¼ cup buttermilk
2 Tbsp butter, unsalted
1 tsp salt
½ cup currants
3 cups self-rising flour, divided
1 egg

Demelza's kind heart means she is always thinking of others. Oftentimes, she makes baskets of saffron buns for the workers at Wheal Leisure and the less fortunate children at the Mellin Cottages. In season one, Demelza and Jinny appear to be making saffron buns at Nampara, and you can catch a glimpse of Jud eating one outside. In Cornwall today, you can still find saffron buns, which yield a lovely mix of sweet and savory flavors, delectable when served warm.

You may be surprised to learn that saffron has been grown in England since the fourteenth century. It was highly valued at the time and used in many different ways—to flavor food and beverage, and also to add color to sauces. Saffron was also used to dye wool and provide pigment for manuscripts. The vibrant saffron threads come from the purple crocus flower, which contains three stigmas that must be harvested with great care, then dried. It takes 14,000 stigmas to make one ounce of saffron, which explains its high cost.

STEPS

1. Soak saffron threads in hot water until the water is cool and ready to use. Set aside.
2. In a standing mixer bowl, combine yeast, sugar, and warm water. Gently stir and allow the yeast to become frothy, about 10 minutes.
3. In a saucepan, warm the buttermilk and butter on medium heat until the butter has melted and the liquid is warm; do not boil. Remove from heat and add saffron threads, the saffron-infused water, salt, and currants. Stir until combined.
4. Turn the mixer on low. Add 1½ cups flour, followed by half of the liquid. Turn off the mixer and scrape down the sides.

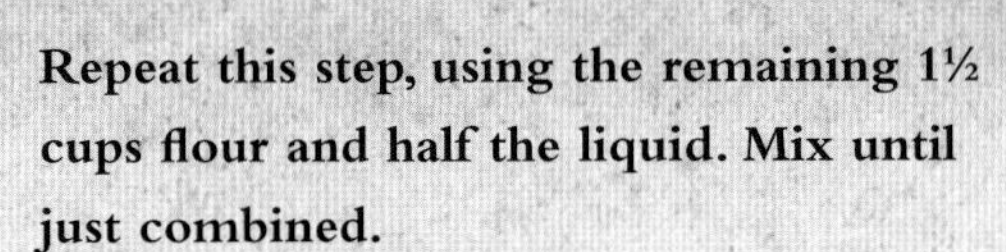

Repeat this step, using the remaining 1½ cups flour and half the liquid. Mix until just combined.

5. On a floured surface, add the dough and knead into a ball.
6. Butter a large mixing bowl, and add the ball of dough. Lay a damp towel over the bowl and store in a warm location for 1½ hours. The dough will double in size.
7. Punch down the dough, and make buns on a floured surface. Place the buns on a cookie sheet and allow them to rest for ½ hour.
8. Set oven to 400 degrees. Cook buns in the oven for 15 minutes.
9. Brush the egg wash on top of the buns and cook for another 3 minutes.
10. Remove from the oven and let the buns cool on a rack.

CORNISH SPLITS

MAKES 8 PIECES

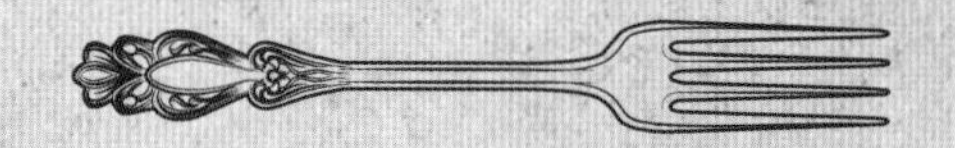

INGREDIENTS

1 tsp dry yeast
2 cups warm milk
1 Tbsp sugar
3⅓ cups all-purpose flour
¼ tsp salt
¼ cup lard, room temperature

Throughout the series, there have been at least three times when either Demelza or Prudie can be seen in the kitchen of Nampara forming little round pieces of dough. If you have read the Poldark novels by Winston Graham, you know what these breads are. If not, you are about to experience a classic and traditional Cornish bread called Cornish splits.

Cornish splits are a rather soft yeast-risen roll. They were usually served during the morning hours for breakfast and sometimes during the afternoon if guests were present. When brought to the table, they were accompanied by fresh fruit preserves or Cornish-style clotted cream. Their name is derived from the fact that you would split them open to add the preserves or cream before eating.

STEPS

1. In a large bowl, whisk the yeast, warm milk, and sugar. Set the bowl side for 10 minutes for the yeast to proof (foam).
2. In a medium bowl, whisk the flour and salt.
3. Add the flour mixture and lard to the proofed mixture and stir to form a dough.
4. Place the dough onto a floured surface and knead for 10 minutes. Place the dough back into the bowl, cover, and let rise for 2 hours in a warm area.
5. Place the dough onto a floured surface and knead for 5 minutes. Portion the dough into 8 pieces and form each into a ball.
6. Line a baking sheet with parchment paper or a silicone sheet.
7. Place the Cornish splits onto the prepared baking sheet and let rise for 1 hour.
8. Preheat your oven to 425 degrees. Place into the oven and bake for 15–20 minutes.
9. Remove from the oven and let cool on a wire rack.

Note: If you want to be a little more authentic, you can bake these in a cast-iron skillet. They will rise and bake into each other, and you can simply pull them apart.

ALMOND CAKE WITH COINTREAU BUTTER SAUCE

MAKES 1 CAKE

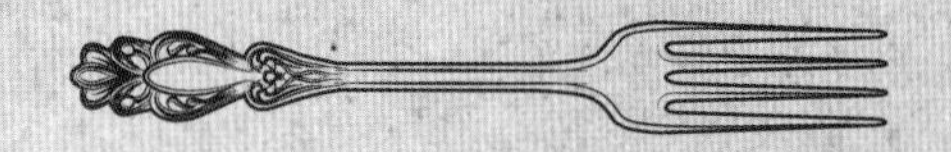

INGREDIENTS

ALMOND CAKE:

1½ cup sugar, plus ½ tsp
Zest of ½ orange
2 eggs, large
½ tsp vanilla paste
1½ tsp almond extract
½ tsp salt
1 cup cake flour
¾ cup melted unsalted buter
¼ cup sliced almonds

COINTREAU BUTTER SAUCE:

8 Tbsp butter, unsalted
½ cup brown sugar, packed
½ cup sugar
⅓ cup heavy cream
3 Tbsp Cointreau
Pinch of salt

Almonds have always been used widely in England, before, during, and after the time of *Poldark*. During medieval times, almonds were ground up finely to create almond milk or used as a thickener for soups and stews. In the Poldark books by Winston Graham, almond cake is mentioned when Ross springs into the kitchen to gather some ale and almond cake before an important discussion with Verity. Like port, almonds cross social lines; Caroline offers to pick up sugar almonds for Uncle Ray to make him feel better, even though he has the sugar sickness.

Our recipe uses almonds in two ways—as an extract and as sugared almonds. Most definitely not a cake for poor Uncle Ray.

STEPS

1. Make the almond cake. Preheat oven at 350 degrees.
2. In a mixing bowl, beat 1½ cup sugar and orange zest together. Add the eggs, one at a time, followed by the vanilla paste, almond extract, and salt.
3. Lower the mixing speed and add the flour, followed by the butter. Fully combine.
4. Grease a 9-inch cake pan. Pour the batter into the cake pan, and sprinkle almonds and the remaining ½ tsp sugar on top.

5. Bake in oven for 40-45 minutes.
6. Remove from oven and slightly cool
7. Make the Cointreau butter sauce. Combine the butter, brown sugar, and sugar in a saucepan over medium heat. Stir often until smooth.
8. Drizzle cream into the butter and sugar mixture, followed by the Cointreau and a pinch of salt. Stirring often, bring to a simmer and cook for 5 minutes.
9. Remove from heat and serve with cake.

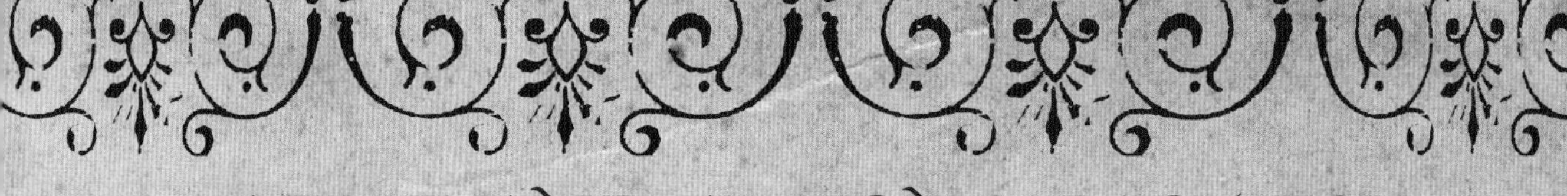

APPLE AND ALMOND PASTIES

MAKES 14–16 PASTIES

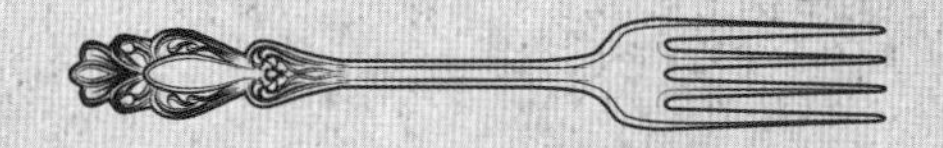

A recipe from one of the first written cookbooks, *A Forme of Cury*, inspires this dish. The almond-filled pastry was baked in honey and wine and was most likely served as a dessert to the guests of King Richard II.

Mead, an ingredient in both the original version and our recipe, is one of the world's oldest alcoholic beverages. It is made from fermented honey and water and was the drink of choice for the Vikings and the Anglo-Saxon warriors. The drink is also well represented in literary classics, from Shakespeare's plays and the ancient oral story of Beowulf to the modern classics of Harry Potter.

In his Poldark books, author Winston Graham mentioned mead as a drink made and consumed by the characters. Mead would have been drunk by the lower classes in the Georgian period, as the ingredients were inexpensive and readily available to most farmers. Characters like Demelza and Jinny would have made the drink for everyday consuming or saved it for celebrations and feasts.

INGREDIENTS

2½ Tbsp butter, unsalted
1 apple, cored and diced
2 Tbsp currants
1 Tbsp sugar
2 tsp ground ginger
Pinch salt
1 7-oz container almond paste
1 puff pastry sheet, thawed
1 egg, beaten
¼ cup honey
¼ cup mead

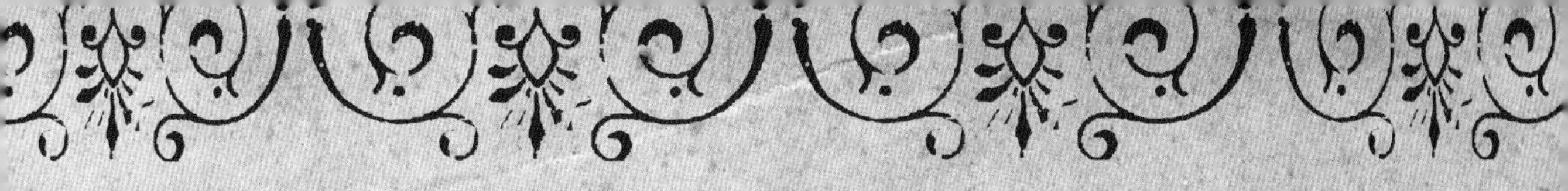

STEPS

1. Preheat the oven to 375 degrees.
2. Melt the butter in a medium saucepan. Add the apple, currants, sugar, ginger, and salt. Once the apples are soft, remove the pan from the heat and cool.
3. In a food processor, add the almond paste and chop until it resembles sand.
4. In a mixing bowl, combine the cooled apple and almond paste. Combine, cover, and store in the refrigerator to chill.
5. Lay the thawed pastry sheet on a lightly floured surface. Roll out the dough until thin, but not so thin that you can see through it. Using a biscuit cutter or a glass, cut out round circles in the pastry.
6. Place 1 heaping tsp apple mix on the round dough, toward the bottom center.
7. Using a beaten egg, brush the outside circumference of the round with the egg wash and fold. Using your hands, press the edges together to seal firmly, forming a half-circle. Place the pastries on a cookie sheet and chill in the refrigerator for at least 30 minutes.
8. Add the honey and mead to a saucepan. Bring the mixture to a boil, skimming off any foam from the top. Reduce the heat to medium-low and let simmer to allow the sauce to thicken.
9. Place the pastry in oven and cook for 15 minutes. Brush the pastries with honey mead and bake for another 15 minutes.
10. Remove from the oven and cool.

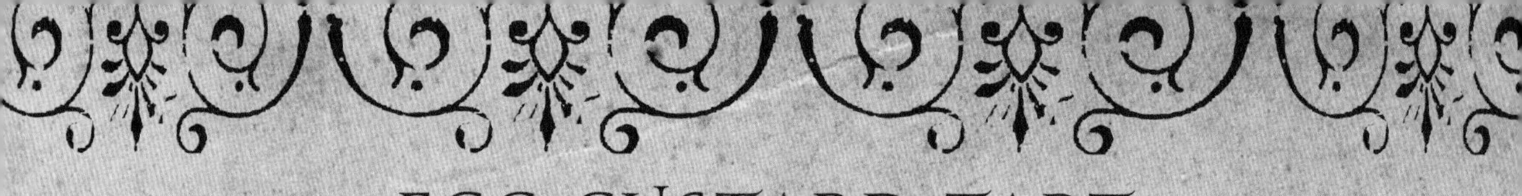

EGG CUSTARD TART

Makes 2 tarts

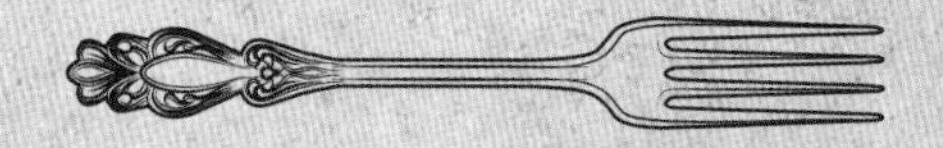

When Verity first visits Nampara to see Demelza in season one, the young wife is so nervous she feels like a serving girl once again in Verity's presence. While sitting awkwardly with Ross and Verity, Demelza looks for any reason to leave the room, and declares that she must check to see if her custard has set. Though we do not know what kind of custard she made, a simple egg custard would have been a possibility, due to its easily accessible ingredients.

INGREDIENTS

3 eggs, plus 3 egg yolks; large and lightly beaten
¾ cup sugar
2½ cups heavy cream
1 Tbsp vanilla paste
Savory Piecrust Dough (page 126)
½ tsp ground nutmeg

STEPS

1. Set the oven at 425 degrees.
2. In a large mixing bowl, beat the eggs, egg yolks (discard the egg whites or save for the next day's breakfast), and sugar. Set aside.
3. In a saucepan on medium heat, warm the cream and vanilla paste. Do not allow the cream to boil, just warm until bubbles form around the sides of the pan.
4. With a whisk, slowly add the cream to the eggs, stirring vigorously to prevent the eggs from cooking from the heat of the cream.
5. Pour the egg and cream mixture through a fine mesh sieve into the piecrusts. Sprinkle evenly with nutmeg.
6. Place the egg custard tarts on a baking sheet and set in the center of the oven.
7. Bake for 10 minutes. Lower the heat to 350 degrees, and continue to bake for another 30 minutes.
8. Remove from the oven and cool. Set in the refrigerator for at least 4 hours or overnight.

Note: Purchase a nutmeg grinder. Once you try the flavor and taste of fresh nutmeg, you will surely not return to using the store-bought kind.

FIG, GOAT CHEESE, AND HONEY TART

MAKES ONE 8X8 TART

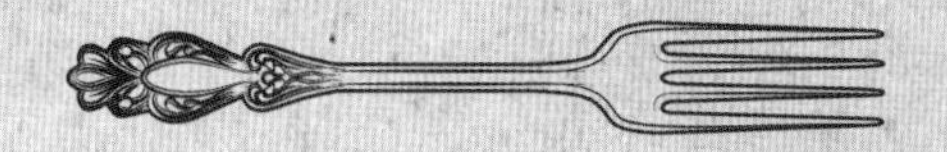

Fig, goat cheese, and honey play major roles in the food of *Poldark*. Figs are almost always shown on the beautifully decorated dinner tables at manors, and goat milk and honey is often used as medicine for the common people. Dr. Enys would prescribe goat milk, along with exercise and fresh air, to the workers in the mine for their lung afflictions. As for us, we find the combination of these ingredients delicious!

INGREDIENTS

DOUGH:

- 7 oz all-purpose flour
- 7 Tbsp butter, unsalted and frozen
- 3½ Tbsp water
- ⅓ tsp salt
- 3 Tbsp sugar, divided
- 1 egg yolk, large
- Zest of 1 orange (about 2 tsp)
- 15 fresh figs, de-stemmed and halved
- ¼ cup brown sugar, packed

CREAM LAYER:

- 16 oz mascarpone cheese
- 4 oz goat cheese
- ¼ cup honey

STEPS

1. Make the dough. On a flat surface, place the flour in a mound and create a well in the middle. Remove the butter from the freezer and grate the butter into the mound.
2. Using your fingers, rub the butter into the flour until it resembles bread crumbs.
3. Add the water, salt, sugar, egg yolk, and orange zest to the flour. Using your hands, mix into the dough.

4. Gently knead the dough twice, press flat, cover in plastic wrap, and chill for at least 2 hours.
5. Prepare the figs. Preheat the oven to broil. Place the figs, cut-side up, on a lined baking sheet. Sprinkle brown sugar over the figs.
6. Broil until the sugar caramelizes, about 5 minutes. Remove from the oven, set aside, and cool.
7. Change the oven temperature to 350 degrees. Roll out the dough on a lightly floured surface until it easily fits the size of the pan, with some overlap, and is approximately ¼ inch thick. We used an 8x8 tart pan, with a removable bottom. Using your fingers, press the dough into the sides and corners of the pan. Using a rolling pin, roll over the dough at the top of the pan for an even edge. Chill the dough in the pan for 30 minutes.
8. Remove the pan from the refrigerator and place in the oven for 30 minutes, cooking until golden. Remove and cool.
9. Make the cream layer. Combine mascarpone and goat cheese until light, followed by honey. Beat until smooth.
10. Prepare the tart by scooping the cream mixture over the cooled tart, using a knife or spatula to spread evenly. Place the figs on top in even rows. Drizzle honey over the top.
11. Chill for at least 30 minutes and serve.

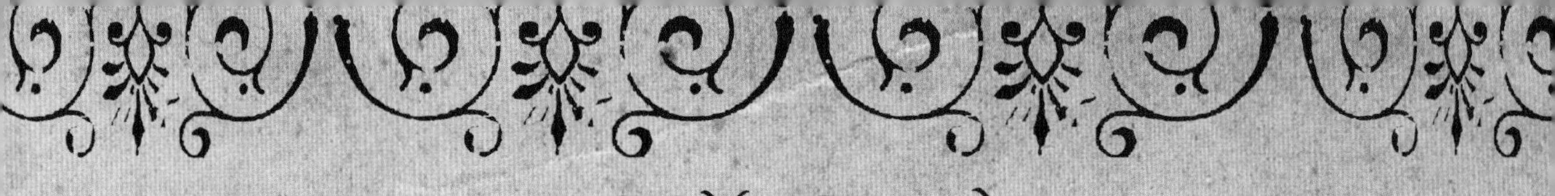

FIGGY 'OBBIN

MAKES 1 PASTRY

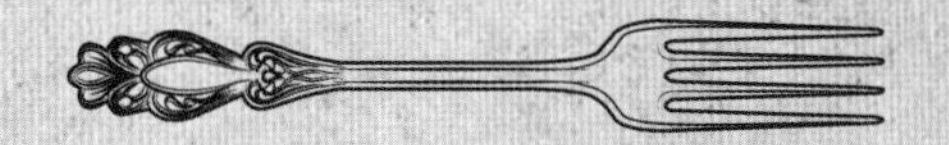

Though its origins are unclear, Figgy 'Obbin is a traditional Cornish sweet. The ingredients would have been easy for Demelza to find and make for her family to enjoy. The word *figgy* is misunderstood by most who live outside of the United Kingdom—it refers to raisins, not figs. We also understand that *'obbin* may mean oven, but don't quote us on it. This simple and delicious treat takes no time to make and is wonderful with a cup of tea.

INGREDIENTS

1 sheet puff pastry, thawed
2 tsp sugar, plus more to sprinkle
1½ cup raisins
Zest of 1 lemon
1 egg, beaten
Buttermilk

STEPS

1. Preheat oven at 350 degrees.
2. On a lightly floured surface, roll out the puff pastry sheet until ½ inch thick.
3. Leaving ½ inch of space at the bottom, sprinkle the rest of the pastry evenly with sugar, raisins, and lemon zest.
4. Starting at the top edge, work your way along, tucking in the pastry to start making the roll. Roll evenly and tight. Seal the bottom edge with egg wash, along with any ends.
5. Transfer to a lined baking sheet. Make slits across the top of the pastry, brush with buttermilk, and sprinkle sugar on top.
6. Bake for 30 minutes. Serve warm.

SOUR MILK CAKE

Makes 1 cake

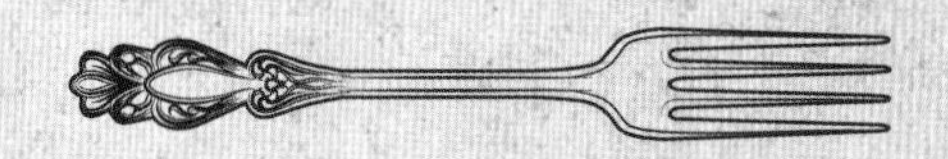

INGREDIENTS

1½ cups all-purpose flour
1 tsp baking powder
¼ tsp baking soda
¼ tsp salt
½ cup butter, softened
1 cup sugar
2 eggs, beaten
1 Tbsp almond extract
½ cup sour milk or buttermilk

It has happened to all of us. You reach into the refrigerator to grab the milk, but it has turned sour! You curse and proceed to pour the milk down the sink. . . . Now, imagine if you lived during the time of *Poldark* without refrigeration; your milk would go sour faster and you can't afford to be throwing food away. What do you do? You make a cake!

Sour milk has been a popular baking ingredient throughout Europe for centuries. In fact, for almost any buttermilk recipe you may have, you can always substitute sour milk (*just don't drink it!*). This is a wonderful single-layer cake, which was often served with fresh fruit and clotted or double cream.

STEPS

1. Preheat your oven to 375 degrees. Line the bottom of a 9-inch round cake pan with parchment paper.
2. In a medium bowl, whisk together the flour, baking powder, baking soda, and salt.
3. In a mixer with the paddle attachment, beat the butter and sugar for 5 minutes. Scrape down the bowl a few times.
4. Add the eggs and beat for 5 minutes. Scrape down the bowl a few times.
5. Beat in half of the flour mixture until just combined.
6. Add the almond extract and sour milk or buttermilk, and beat for 5 minutes. Scrape down the bowl a few times.
7. Add the remaining flour mixture and beat until just combined.
8. Spoon the batter into the prepared pan. Place into the oven and bake for 30–35 minutes.
9. Remove from the oven and let cool in the pan for 5 minutes. Remove from the pan and let cool on a wire rack.

HEVVA CAKE

Makes 1 cake

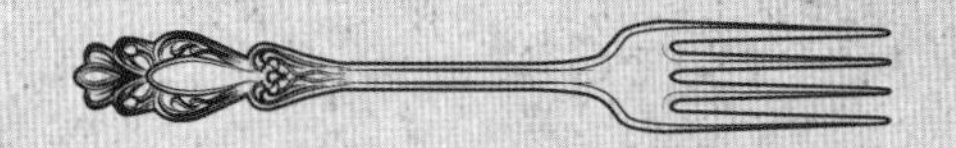

INGREDIENTS

- 1½ lb all-purpose flour
- ¼ tsp salt
- ¾ tsp ground ginger
- ¾ tsp cinnamon
- ½ cup sugar, plus more for finishing
- 8 oz unsalted butter; cold, cut into pats
- 1¼ cup currants
- 1 cup water

Cornish hevva, or heavy cake, is a traditional teatime treat of the pilchard (sardine) fishing communities of Cornwall. In season one, the fishing heur (lookout person) yells "heva heva" as soon as he sees the signs of the pilchards. Once the heur made his announcement, the fishermen's wives would quickly return home and bake this treat for their hard-working husbands as a way to celebrate the bounty. These pilchards, salted and stored, would last the communities through the winter, which was important for those who had little.

In one of our favorite scenes, Aunt Agatha learns that George did not tell her about Clowance's christening, and she does not hold back from expressing her dismay. Not only did she lose time with Ross and the family, she also missed out on an opportunity to drink port and eat heavy cake! Here, our cake is scored with lines to resemble a fishing net.

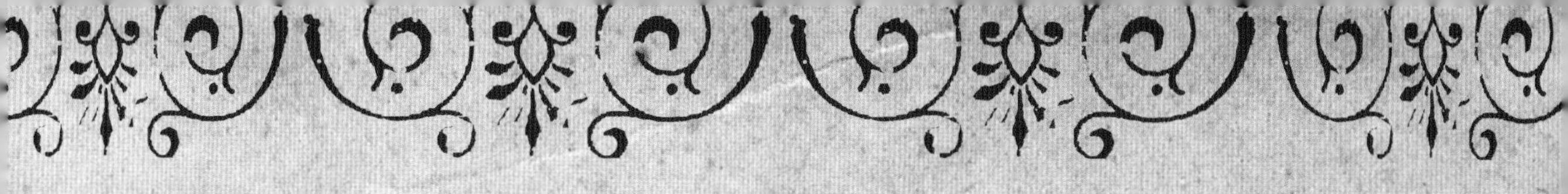

STEPS

1. Preheat oven to 375 degrees. Grease a large baking tray.
2. Combine flour, salt, ginger, cinnamon, and ½ cup sugar in a large mixing bowl.
3. Add butter to the mix and rub it into the dry mixture until it resembles bread crumbs.
4. Add the currants and water to the mixing bowl, and combine well.
5. Roll out the dough on a floured surface to the shape of the tray, with a thickness of slightly less than 1 inch.
6. Transfer the dough to the cookie sheet. Using a knife, score the dough in a diamond pattern to resemble a fishing net. Sprinkle extra sugar over the dough.
7. Bake for 25–30 minutes.

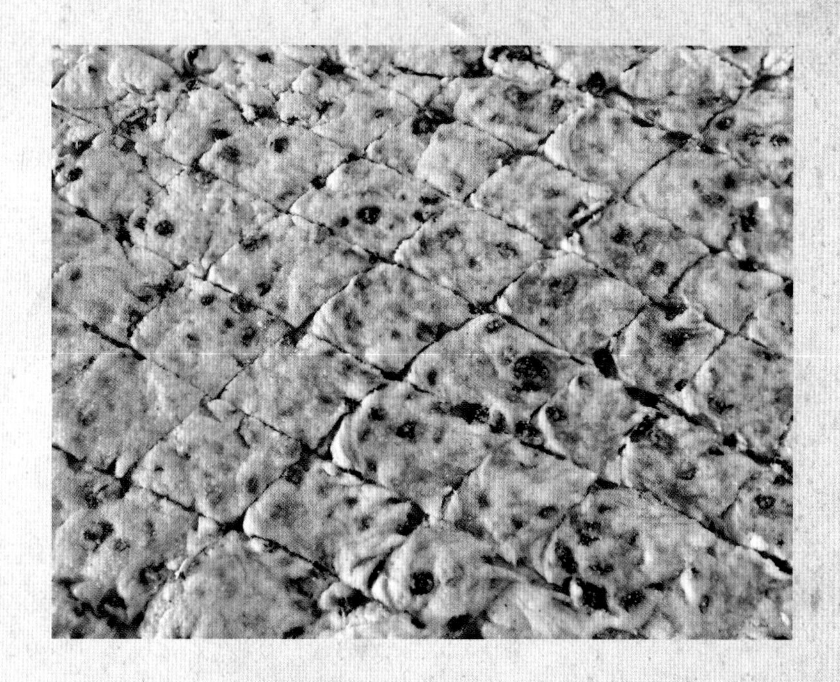

MILK CAKE

MAKES 1 CAKE

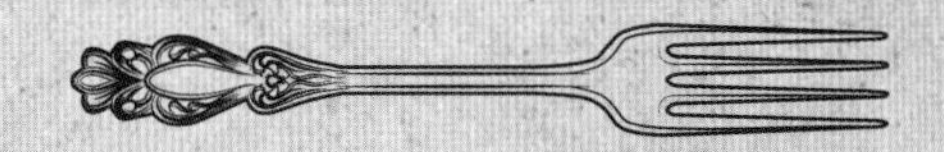

INGREDIENTS

4 eggs, beaten
2 cups sugar
1 tsp vanilla
2¼ cups all-purpose flour
2¼ tsp baking powder
1¼ cups milk
10 Tbsp butter, softened

During the eighteenth century, there was, of course, no refrigeration. Because of this, cooks and chefs had to be quite imaginative when it came to preparing dishes as resources were scarce and wasting food was tantamount to offensiveness. One of the quickest food staples to go bad was dairy, so when there was a little too much milk, a milk cake would be prepared.

This simple cake can be made in very little time. There were usually two ways it was presented—first, as a simple slice to ease a sweet craving; and second, as a hefty slice with some double cream and fresh fruit or fruit preserves if there was company or visitors.

STEPS

1. Preheat your oven to 350 degrees. Line the bottom of a 9-inch round cake pan with parchment paper.
2. In a mixer with the paddle attachment, beat the eggs and sugar for 5 minutes. Remember to scrape down the bowl a few times.
3. Add the vanilla and beat for 3 minutes.
4. In a medium bowl, whisk the flour and baking powder.
5. In a small saucepan, heat the milk and butter just until the butter melts.
6. Stir the flour mixture into the egg mixture, but do not beat it in. Stir the milk mixture into the batter just until smooth.
7. Spoon the batter into the prepared cake pan. Place into the oven and bake for 40–45 minutes.
8. Remove from the oven and let cool in the pan for 10 minutes. Remove the milk cake from the pan and let cool on a wire rack.

ORANGE CHEESECAKE WITH A SHORTBREAD CRUST

MAKES 1 CAKE

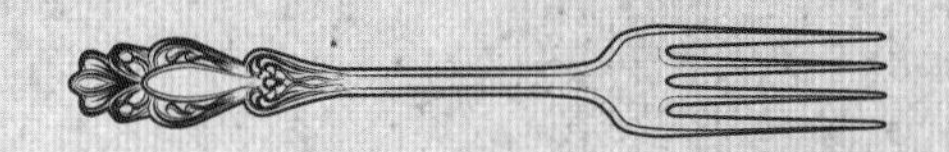

In season one, Jud is caught stealing a cake that Demelza has just made. The cake he runs away with looks a lot like a cheesecake—and there would have been a good chance that it was. Cheesecake has been made for hundreds of years, way before Demelza. Often referred to as *sambocade*, it was a cheese tart sweetened not with vanilla but with elderflower.

We added orange to this dessert as a nod to Dr. Enys. As a doctor, he was aware of the nutritional value of oranges for the miners. Since miners generally came from little means, their diet lacked nutrition—not to mention they did not get a healthy dose of vitamin C.

INGREDIENTS

10 oz shortbread cookies
2 lb cream cheese, room temperature
1 cup sugar, plus 2 Tbsp divided
4 large eggs
¼ cup whole milk
2 Tbsp orange liquor or orange juice, divided
Zest of 1 orange (about 1½ Tbsp)
2 cups sour cream
Orange slices, to garnish

STEPS

1. Preheat the oven to 325 degrees.
2. Blend shortbread cookies in a food processor. It will make about 1¼ cup crumbs.
3. Press cookie crumbs into the bottom and sides of an 8-inch springform pan.
4. Place the cream cheese into a standing mixer bowl. Turn the mixer on medium-high and whip the cream cheese until light and airy.
5. Add 1 cup sugar and beat until combined and very smooth.
6. Crack the eggs into a separate bowl. With the mixer on, slowly beat in the eggs one at a time. Stop the mixer between eggs to scrape down the sides and bottom of bowl.
7. Add in the milk and 1 Tbsp orange liqueur and the orange zest. Beat until smooth.

8. Pour mixture into the prepared crust. Place the springform pan onto a cookie sheet in case of spillage. Cook in the oven for 1 hour.
9. Combine the sour cream, the remaining 2 Tbsp sugar, and remaining 1 Tbsp orange liquor in a small bowl.
10. Remove the cheesecake from the oven, but keep the oven on. The cake will still have some jiggle to it, which is the way it should be. Let the cheesecake cool for 10 minutes, and then gently add the sour cream mixture to the top of the cake. Put it back in the oven for another 10 minutes.
11. Remove from the oven and let it cool completely. Store in the refrigerator, covered, for at least 6 hours or overnight. Garnish with orange slices.

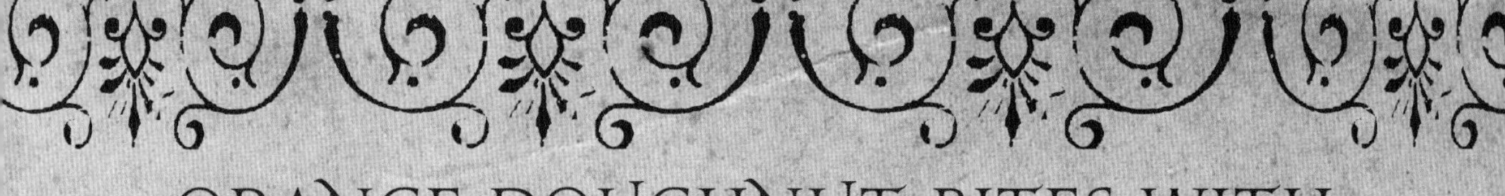

ORANGE DOUGHNUT BITES WITH STOUT CHOCOLATE DIPPING SAUCE

Makes 8–10 doughnuts

Doughnuts have a long European history, starting most likely with the Dutch. Their version, *oliekoecken* (oil or fried cakes) was somewhat sticky, had ingredients like dried fruit and spices, and was consumed during the time of Christmas through to the Twelfth Night. As they made their way throughout the rest of Europe, the cooking techniques changed as well as the shape, size, and occasion when they were consumed.

The 1800 English cookbook *The Receipt Book of Baroness Elizabeth Dimsdale* called for "dow nuts" made using sugar, eggs, nutmeg, butter, and yeast that were formed into nut-size shapes. Doughnuts became so popular with children in England that the dessert at times replaced the traditional pancake on the ancient feast day of Shrove Tuesday.

During the time of *Poldark*, doughnuts with candied orange were sometimes packed with sailors when they went out to sea as a way to prevent scurvy, a vitamin-C deficiency often associated with the inability of sailors to access fresh fruits and vegetables. Though scurvy is rare today, *Poldark* highlights how serious this ailment was, especially with the miners and the poor. Even Dr. Enys suffered from it while being held in France.

INGREDIENTS

ORANGE DOUGHNUT BITES:

8 Tbsp butter, unsalted
1 cup orange juice, fresh
¼ cup sugar
¼ tsp salt
1 cup self-rising flour
3 eggs, large
1 egg yolk, large
Zest of 1 orange (about 1 Tbsp)
Neutral-flavored oil

STOUT CHOCOLATE DIPPING SAUCE:

1½ cup stout (we used Guinness)
2 cups sugar
1 cup semisweet chocolate chips
1 tsp vanilla paste
⅛ tsp salt

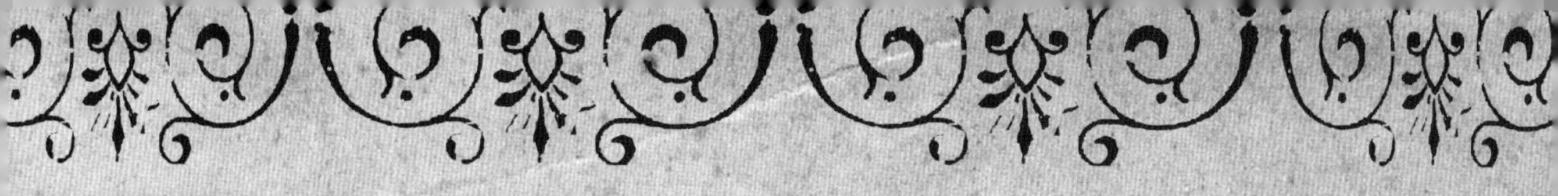

STEPS

1. Make the orange doughnut bites. In a saucepan, combine the butter, orange juice, sugar, and salt over medium heat. Once the liquid reaches a rolling boil, remove the pan from the heat.
2. Blend in the flour. Using a wooden spoon, quickly stir the mixture until it is absorbed and a thick dough begins to form.
3. Return the pan to medium heat and stir the dough continuously for 2 minutes.
4. Remove the pan from the heat and add the dough to a mixing bowl on a stand mixer, with a paddle attachment. Let the dough cool slightly so that it does not cook the eggs during the next step.
5. Turn the mixer on to medium. Add one egg at a time and the separated egg yolk, and mix until thick and glossy, about 4 minutes. Add the orange zest and beat until smooth. Refrigerate the dough for 30 minutes.
6. In a large saucepan or fryer, add enough oil to fill the pan about a third of the way. Heat oil over medium heat until it reaches 375 degrees. Working in batches, use a small scoop to drop donuts into the hot oil.
7. Cook the doughnuts, turning as needed to avoid burning, about 3½–4 minutes.
8. Drain on paper towels.
9. Make the stout chocolate dipping sauce. In a saucepan, combine all the ingredients. Bring the liquid to a boil and reduce the heat until thickened, about 5 minutes. Dip away.

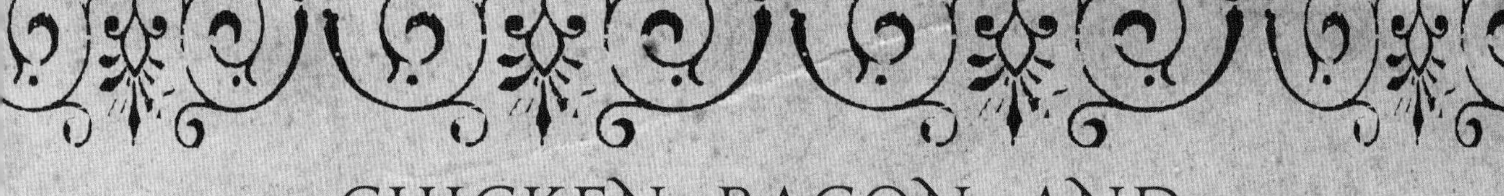

CHICKEN, BACON, AND FENNEL PIE

Makes 1 pie

INGREDIENTS

- 1 sprig fresh sage
- 2 cups chicken stock
- 1½ lb chicken thighs, boneless and skinless
- 1 Tbsp olive oil
- 3 cups fennel; peeled, thinly sliced, cored and greens removed (we used a mandolin)
- 1 large sweet onion. thinly sliced
- 3 cloves garlic, minced
- 4 slices thick-cut bacon
- 7 eggs, large
- 1 tsp ground ginger
- 1 tsp salt
- 1 tsp pepper
- Savory Piecrust Dough (page 126)

The inspiration for this dish comes from a fourteenth-century German recipe. The original dish featured grilled chicken, chopped into bite sizes and combined with eggs, ground ginger, anise, and saffron, and then baked in a shell. This recipe and concept spread around Europe, making its way into England. By 1747, many cookbook authors, including English author Hannah Glasse, made their own versions of chicken and egg pie. The people of Cornwall would add their own spin, using ingredients that were most available to them—which most certainly would have included bacon.

STEPS

1. Place the sage and chicken stock in a saucepan on medium heat. Once the liquid begins to boil, add the chicken and cover. Cook for 15 minutes. Remove the chicken from the liquid, cool, and chop into bite sizes. Set aside.
2. In a sauté pan, heat the olive oil on medium heat. Add the fennel and onion, followed by the garlic. Once soft, remove the vegetables and set aside.
3. Cook the slices of bacon until crispy, but not burnt. Remove from heat, and place on paper towels until cool. Roughly chop and set aside.
4. Preheat the oven at 400 degrees.
5. In a large mixing bowl, whisk the eggs. Add in the cooled chicken and vegetables to combine.
6. Add the ginger, salt, pepper, and bacon, and stir. Pour the mixture into your prepared pie shell. Place your pie pan on a cookie pan to prevent any spillage.
7. Place into the oven for 35 minutes. Slightly cool, and serve.

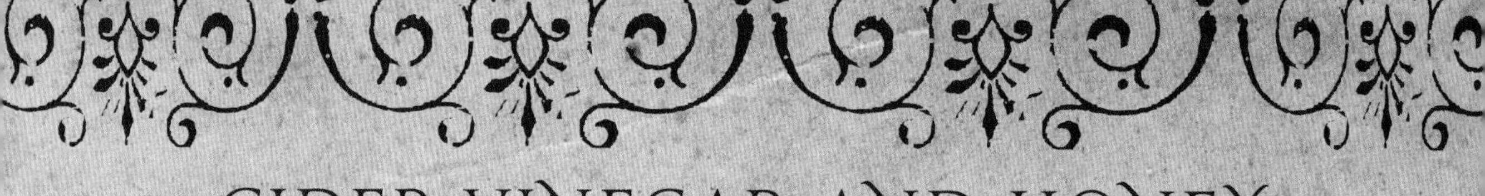

CIDER VINEGAR AND HONEY CHICKEN

SERVES 4

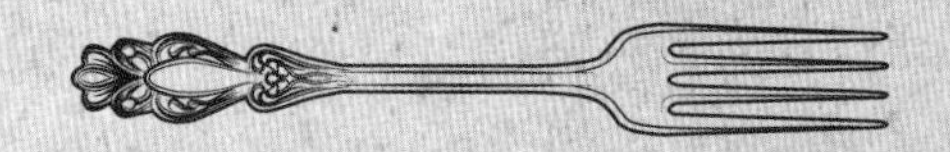

INGREDIENTS

2 chicken breasts; halved, boneless, and skinless
1 tsp salt
½ tsp ground black pepper
1 Tbsp vegetable oil
2 Tbsp apple cider vinegar
3 Tbsp honey
1 Tbsp minced basil

Here's a simple fact of nature: if you live anywhere where apples grow, you will make apple cider vinegar. And if you have apples, you will have bees, which means you will have honey. This very simple Cider Vinegar and Honey Chicken ensures you'll never go a day without a delicious meal.

One thing is for certain, especially when you consider the food of *Poldark*: just because you were a "bluenose" (rich person) doesn't mean you ate better. The food from the homesteads and boardinghouses was quite delicious and, by today's standards, much healthier. Back in the day, this dish used the breast of whatever fowl was available; for simplicity, we use chicken. Though this wasn't normal dinner fare, it was a popular choice for festive occasions such as weddings, birthdays, or holidays.

STEPS

1. Wipe the chicken breasts of any excess moisture. Sprinkle the breasts with salt and pepper.
2. In a large skillet, heat the oil over medium heat. Add the chicken breasts and cook for 5–7 minutes per side (depending on the thickness of the breasts). You want the breasts to be 160 degrees on a meat thermometer. Remove the breasts from the pan and keep warm.
3. Into the pan, stir the apple cider vinegar, honey, and basil. Cook for 1 minute.
4. Place the chicken breasts back into the pan and cook a few minutes on each side.
5. Remove the chicken breasts to serving plates, spoon some sauce over them, and serve.

CREAMED PHEASANT

SERVES 4

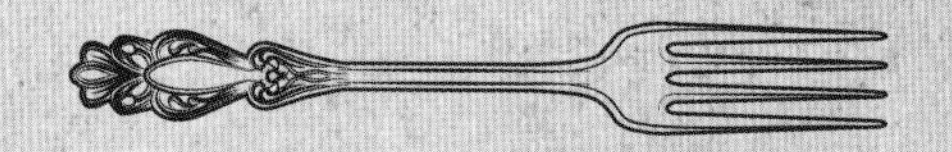

INGREDIENTS

2 Tbsp butter
1 onion, peeled and chopped
4 cloves garlic, peeled and minced
¼ cup chicken stock
4 chicken breasts; boneless, skinless, and chopped
1 tsp salt
½ tsp ground black pepper
2 cups Cornish Cream of Mushroom Soup (page 146)
½ cup buttermilk
1 loaf Brown Soda Bread (page 84) or rice, to serve

As any fan of *Poldark* is well aware, pheasant was one of the favorite fowls at the dinner table. Pheasant would often be hunted by the villagers, and when not brought home to be prepared for a meal, they would be sold on the streets of Cornwall or Truro. At the manors, pheasants were roasted and served whole (including the head); at the homesteads, it would be incorporated into a dish that today would be considered a casserole.

Though you cannot readily buy pheasant at your local market, you can still enjoy this dish by using chicken.

STEPS

1. In a large saucepan, melt the butter over medium heat. Add the onion and garlic, and cook for 5 minutes.
2. Stir in the chicken stock, chicken, salt, and pepper, and cook for 10 minutes.
3. In a medium bowl, whisk the mushroom soup and buttermilk. Stir the mixture into the chicken and cook for 10 minutes.
4. Serve over brown soda bread or rice.

Note: If you don't want to make mushroom soup from scratch, you can use a good-quality cream of mushroom soup from your local market.

HARD CIDER CHICKEN

SERVES 4

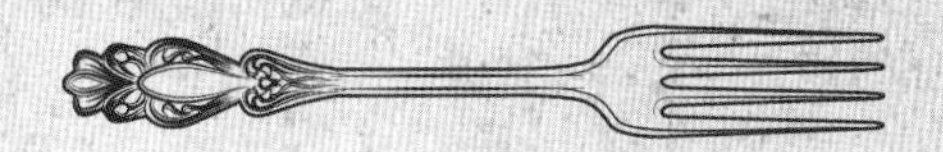

INGREDIENTS

4 chicken leg/thigh portions
2 tsp dry mustard
½ tsp salt
¼ tsp ground black pepper
1 cup hard cider
1 Tbsp melted butter
2 Tbsp honey

It doesn't matter what era it may be—when it comes to hard cider, no one can beat the one made by the people of the United Kingdom. Not only is hard cider still one of the most popular adult beverages today, on a per capita basis no one in the world drinks more of it. And as the *Poldark* kitchens prove, people loved to use it in their cooking during Georgian times. You can find hard cider in the liquor department of most markets.

Whereas the manors loved to bring out whole roasted fowls to the dinner tables, in the boardinghouses or homesteads, the bird was usually cut up and cooked (like most of us do today). In this recipe, we use the leg/thigh portion of the bird. If Hard Cider Chicken were to be prepared at Nampara, it would be grilled over an open flame in the garden—but you can simply grill yours in the oven!

STEPS

1. Remove any excess fat from the chicken.
2. In a small bowl, whisk the dry mustard, salt, pepper, hard cider, butter, and honey.
3. Place the chicken portions in a shallow dish and pour the marinade on top. Turn the chicken a few times to coat.
4. Let the chicken marinate for 1 hour at room temperature. If you leave it for over 1 hour, put it in the refrigerator.
5. Preheat your oven to 350 degrees. Place the chicken in a large skillet and pour the marinade over it. Place into the oven and cook for 1 hour (depending on the size of the leg/thigh portions), basting often. Your chicken should be at 160 degrees on a meat thermometer.
6. Remove from the oven and serve.

CORNISH LAMB LOAF

SERVES 4

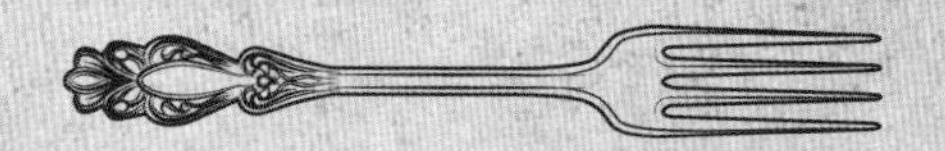

INGREDIENTS

- 1 cup fresh bread crumbs (Cornish Splits would be perfect, page 90)
- ¼ cup beef stock
- ¼ cup ale
- 1½ lb ground lamb
- ½ lb ground pork
- 1 onion, peeled and minced
- 1 cup minced greens (spinach, kale, chard. etc.)
- ¼ cup minced parsley
- 1 egg, beaten
- 2 tsp salt
- 1 tsp ground black pepper

We have all seen Ross, Francis, or George riding their horses across the beautiful Cornish countryside, but what we don't usually see is the livestock that provided for the locals. Although cows were not as popular back then, sheep (lamb) was a main food source, and as a result it is featured in many classic Cornish meat dishes.

Cornish Lamb Loaf would be considered a meatloaf by today's culinary standards. In the eighteenth century, it would often be prepared by steaming and then served with what was known simply as a brown sauce, which was really any sauce that was indeed brown and made from leftover meats or organs. Not really too appetizing! In this adaptation of Cornish Lamb Loaf, we will bake it and serve it with either an herb tomato sauce (readily available at all markets) or . . . ketchup (yes, very un-Poldark-like).

STEPS

1. Preheat your oven to 350 degrees. Line the bottom of a 9x5 loaf pan with parchment paper and lightly oil the sides.
2. In a large bowl, combine all the ingredients and, using your hands, mix until very well combined.
3. Spoon the mixture into the prepared loaf pan. Place the pan in the oven and bake for 90 minutes or until it reaches 165 degrees on a meat thermometer.
4. Remove from the oven and let cool in the pan for 10 minutes. Then, remove from the pan, slice, and serve.

SHEPHERD'S PIE

SERVES 4

There is an adage that goes, "Wherever you find a pasture, you will find a version of shepherd's pie." This may very well be true, and the cliffside pastures of Cornwall, laden with livestock, did in fact influence this shepherd's pie, which is loaded with fresh flavors of the region. This version doesn't have a crust; it simply cooks on its own.

INGREDIENTS

1 Tbsp lard
2 carrots, peeled and diced
2 parsnips, peeled and diced
1 onion, peeled and minced
1 tsp salt
½ tsp ground black pepper
1 lb ground lamb
1 Tbsp butter
2 Tbsp all-purpose flour
2 cups beef stock
4 sprigs fresh thyme
2 cups mashed potatoes
1 egg, beaten

STEPS

1. Preheat your oven to 400 degrees. In a medium cast-iron skillet, heat the lard over medium heat.
2. Add the carrots, parsnips, onion, salt, and pepper, and cook for 5 minutes.
3. Add the ground lamb, butter, and flour, and cook for 5 minutes, while stirring.
4. Stir in the beef stock and thyme, and bring to a boil. Reduce the heat to a simmer and cook for about 10 minutes so the sauce thickens to a gravy.
5. In a medium bowl, whisk the mashed potatoes and beaten egg. Either spread the mashed potatoes or pipe them on top of the shepherd's pie.
6. Place into the oven and bake for 20 minutes.
7. Remove from the oven and let cool slightly before serving.

Note: To make authentic shepherd's pie, use ground lamb, though you can modernize it by adding beef. The big difference between shepherd's pie and mutton pie (page 124) is that you may only use mutton or lamb, and not beef, for the latter.

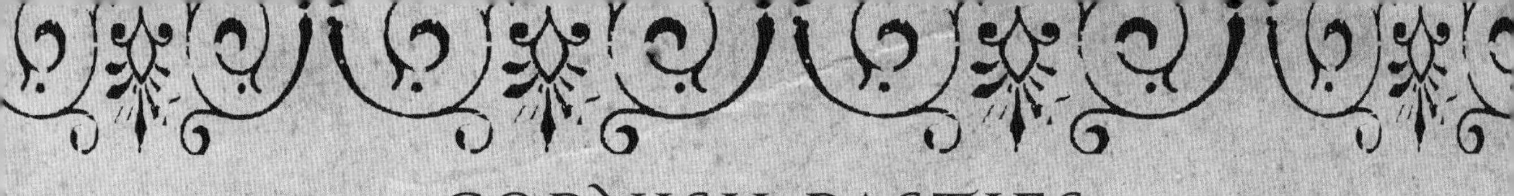

CORNISH PASTIES

MAKES 4

In the annals of British cookery, there is no dish more associated with Cornwall than their famed Cornish pasties. In fact, in 2011, Cornish pasties were granted PGI status (protected geographical indication) in Europe, meaning you cannot sell Cornish pasties or call your dish "Cornish pasties" if they are not made in Cornwall, England. Since the popularity of *Poldark* and the influx of tourism into Cornwall, Cornish pasties are becoming one of the most popular British dishes in the world.

So, what are they? Cornish pasties are a savory hand-held meat pie, with a crust created from a Cornish pastry dough. During the Georgian era, it was a favorite dish among miners. It gained popularity throughout the United Kingdom when the Cornish mines started to close and the miners went to work in other parts of the Commonwealth.

INGREDIENTS

PASTRY DOUGH:

4 cups all-purpose flour
1½ tsp salt
6 Tbsp lard
¼ cup butter, chilled and diced
1 cup cold water

FILLING:

1 lb ground beef
1 large potato, peeled and diced
1 onion, peeled and minced
1½ tsp salt
1 tsp ground black pepper
1 Tbsp butter
1 egg yolk
1 tsp water

STEPS

1. Prepare the pastry dough. In a large bowl, combine the flour, salt, lard, and butter. Using a pastry blender, cut the lard and butter into the flour until the texture is crumbly.
2. Stir in the cold water to form a dough. Depending on the humidity of your kitchen, you may need a little more water. Wrap the dough in plastic and chill for at least 1 hour before rolling out.
3. Preheat your oven to 350 degrees. Line a baking sheet with parchment paper or a silicone sheet.
4. Prepare the filling. In a medium bowl, combine the ground beef, potato, onion,

salt, and pepper. Mix thoroughly with your hands. Set the bowl aside.

5. Divide your Cornish pastry dough into 4 equal portions. On a floured surface, roll the pastry dough into a circle with the same thickness as a piecrust.
6. Place a quarter of the filling slightly off-center on the dough. Place some butter atop the filling. Fold the dough over the filling into a half-moon shape and seal the edges by pinching them. Place the Cornish pasties onto the prepared baking sheet and crimp the edges with the tines of a fork.
7. In a small bowl, whisk the egg yolk and water. Brush the top of each pasty with the egg wash.
8. With a sharp knife, make a few shallow slits in the top of each of the pasties (this will act as a steam vent when baking). Place into the oven and bake for 1 hour.
9. Remove from the oven and let cool on a wire rack before eating.

Note: You can make the pastry dough (steps 1–4) in a food processor—and we won't tell Demelza. Simply place the flour, salt, lard, and butter in the processor and pulse until crumbly. With the machine running, add the water until a dough is formed.

PLOUGH PUDDING

Serves 6–8

Dating back to the early fifteenth century, Plough Monday is the feast celebrated the first Monday after Twelfth Night (January 5). To celebrate the new harvest season, the farmers would eat a hearty meal of plough pudding, a traditional Norfolk dish of steamed pudding with meat.

In season two, the Poldark family gathers at Trenwith to celebrate the harvest with a traditional Cornish ceremony called "Crying the Neck." Francis holds a neck of wheat over his head, and along with the other participants declares a successful harvest.

INGREDIENTS

CRUST:

- 6 Tbsp vegetable shortening, plus extra for greasing
- 2 cups all-purpose flour
- 1 Tbsp baking powder
- 1 tsp salt
- ½ cup cold water

FILLINGS:

- ½ cup diced apples
- ½ cup diced Yukon gold potatoes
- 1 lb sweet pork sausage, bulk (not in the casing)
- ½ teaspoon black pepper
- Pinch salt
- 1 Tbsp fresh sage, finely chopped
- 3 slices thick cut bacon, uncooked and chopped
- ½ cup sweet onions, chopped
- 2½ Tbsp brown sugar, tightly packed

STEPS

1. Prepare the crust. Generously grease the pudding basin with shortening and set aside.
2. Combine flour, baking powder, and salt into a mixing bowl.
3. Add 6 Tbsp shortening to the flour and rub together until the mixture resembles bread crumbs. Slowly add the water until the dough comes together.
4. Knead the dough on a floured surface until combined. Shape into a ball and

cut the dough into 3 pieces. Tightly wrap the dough in plastic wrap and place in the refrigerator until chilled.

5. Remove the chilled dough from the refrigerator. Combine 2 of the rounds together and roll out on a lightly floured surface until ⅛-inch thick and somewhat round, big enough to fully line the inside of the basin. With the flattened dough in your hands, carefully hold over the basin. Drop the center of the dough in first, followed by the sides. To remove air bubbles, press the dough down in the center, followed by the sides. Trim any dough that is not even with the top of the basin. Use the trimmed dough to fill in tears or gaps.
6. Prepare the filling. Parboil the apple and potatoes until a knife can pierce them easily. Remove from the hot water and let cool.
7. In a mixing bowl, combine the bulk sausage, pepper, salt, and sage. Once fully combined, press the mixture evenly into the dough on the bottom and sides.
8. In a separate bowl, combine the apple, potatoes, bacon, onions, and brown sugar. Add into the center of the pudding basin. You may need to press down on it a bit to make sure it is even with the top.
9. Roll out the remaining 1 piece of dough to fit the top of the pudding. To seal, brush some water onto the dough in the pudding basin and firmly seal the two pieces by pressing together. Trim off any unnecessary dough.
10. Cover the top with parchment paper, followed by aluminum foil. Wrap kitchen twine around the top circumference of the basin, locking the foil and paper into place. Trim any excess materials to prevent water (in the next step) from getting into the basin.
11. Put the basin into a large pot. Pour water into the pot until it reaches ¾ of the way up the basin. Avoid getting water on top of the basin. Boil the water with the basin in the pot for 4 hours. As the water starts to evaporate, fill it up with hot water from a kettle. This long process requires your attention, but it will be worth it.
12. After 4 hours, carefully remove the basin from the pot and let cool. Discard the parchment paper and foil. With a sharp paring knife, go around the sides ever so gently to loosen, being careful to not puncture the golden dough. Place a plate on the top of the basin and flip it over.
13. Slice and enjoy.

Note: We used a 0.95-quart pudding basin

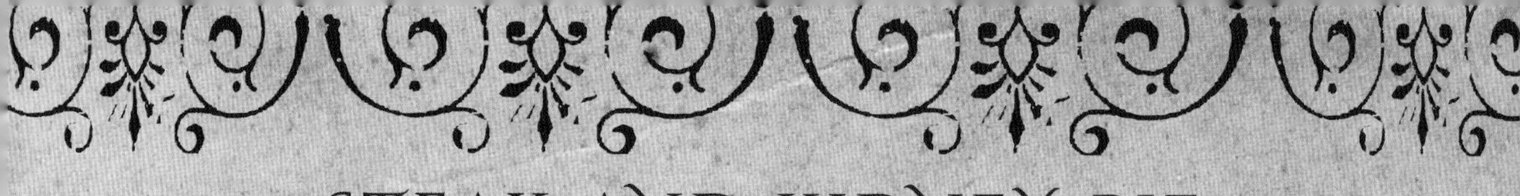

STEAK AND KIDNEY PIE

SERVES 4

INGREDIENTS

- 1 lb lean beef, chopped
- ½ lb beef kidneys, rinsed under cold water
- ½ cup all-purpose flour
- 2 Tbsp lard
- ½ tsp salt
- ¼ tsp ground black pepper
- 1 onion, chopped
- 4 parsnips, peeled and chopped
- 3 cups beef stock
- Savory Piecrust Dough (page 126)
- 2 cups mashed potatoes

It doesn't matter if it is Prudie, Demelza, a cook at the Red Lion, or one of the personal chefs at Trenwith—there is one certainty when it comes to Poldark: a Steak and Kidney Pie will be served at least once a week!

Why was this one of the most popular diets meals the time? It was cheap and easy to make, and it tasted good! To make this dish, any cut of beef could be used—whether a cheap and tough cut at the Red Lion or at Nampara, or a leaner cut at Trenwith. Though a savory pie, it did not usually have a top crust. Instead, mashed potatoes were either spread on or, in the case of a party at a manor, pipped on in a design.

STEPS

1. In a medium bowl, dredge the beef and kidneys with flour.
2. In a medium skillet, heat the lard over medium heat. Add the dredged beef and kidneys and cook for 5 minutes. Remove the beef and kidneys with a slotted spoon and set aside.
3. Into the skillet, add the salt, pepper, onion, and parsnips, and cook for 7 minutes.
4. Return the beef and kidneys to the skillet and stir in the beef stock. Bring the mixture to a simmer and cook for 35 minutes.
5. Preheat your oven to 350 degrees. Remove the pan from the heat and let cool for 30 minutes. It will thicken as it cools.

6. Roll out the Savory Piecrust Dough to fit an 8-to-9-inch pie plate. Place the piecrust into the pie plate, making sure it overlaps a little as it will shrink as it bakes. Using the tines of a fork, poke holes all over the bottom and sides of the piecrust. Don't worry, you can't poke too many.
7. Place into the oven and bake for 25 minutes.
8. Remove from the oven. Do not turn the oven off. Spoon the steak and kidney filling into the piecrust. Either spread or pipe (using a star tip) the mashed potatoes over the top of the pie.
9. Place into the oven and bake for about 15 minutes or just until the potatoes get some color.
10. Remove from the oven and let rest for about 10 minutes before serving.

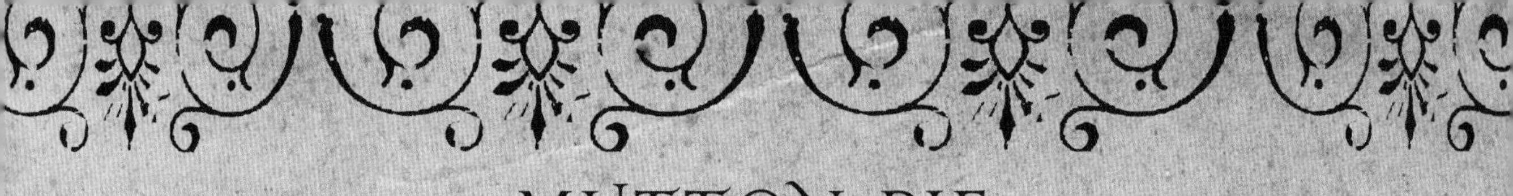

MUTTON PIE

SERVES 4

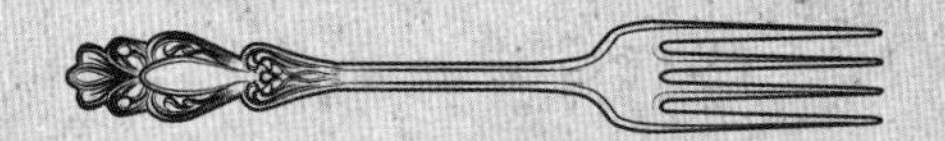

Mutton pie is a quintessential old-world English savory pie. Mutton pie has always been a boardinghouse and pub favorite—whether during the era of *Poldark* or today. It was also a favorite meal served at the manors—but there it was usually called "lamb pie," and the topping was a crown of piped-on mashed potatoes instead of a crust.

Mutton refers to the meat of an aged sheep. Texture-wise, it is more tough, and flavor-wise, it is more gamey. Mutton costs much less than lamb and was thus considered a "peasant" meat. At the homesteads, mutton often came from an old sheep that could no longer perform its farm duties.

For this version of mutton pie, we will prepare it as they would have at the Red Lion, with a top and bottom crust.

INGREDIENTS

- 2 Savory Piecrust Doughs (page 126)
- ¼ cup vegetable oil
- 1 lb lamb meat (mutton is not usually available at markets)
- ¼ cup all-purpose flour
- ½ tsp salt
- 1 tsp ground black pepper
- ¼ tsp ground allspice
- 1 onion, peeled and chopped
- 1 parsnip, peeled and chopped
- 2 potatoes, peeled and diced
- 1 carrot, peeled and chopped
- ¼ cup apple cider vinegar
- ½ cup port wine
- 1 Tbsp heavy cream
- 1 egg yolk, beaten

STEPS

1. Line the bottom of a 9-inch pie plate with the first Savory Piecrust Dough and set aside. Roll out the second piece of dough so it can fit over the pie. Wrap the second piece in plastic and chill until ready to use.
2. In a medium skillet, heat the oil over medium heat.

3. Add the lamb meat to the skillet. As you are browning it, stir in the flour. Remove the lamb meat with a slotted spoon and set aside.
4. Into the skillet, add the salt, pepper, allspice, onion, parsnip, potatoes, and carrot, and cook for 5 minutes.
5. Stir the vinegar into the pan, scraping the bottom to deglaze. Place the lamb back into the skillet and add the port. Bring to a simmer and cook for 10 minutes.
6. Preheat your oven to 350 degrees. Remove the skillet from the heat and let cool for 10 minutes. It will thicken as it cools.
7. Spoon the lamb mixture into the prepared piecrust. Place the top crust over the pie. Moisten the rim of the crust with some water and pinch to seal the circumference of the crust. With a sharp paring knife, make a few shallow slits in the top crust to act as steam vents.
8. In a small bowl, whisk the heavy cream and egg yolk until smooth. Brush the top of the pie with the egg wash.
9. Place into the oven and bake for 40 minutes.
10. Remove from the oven and let cool slightly before serving.

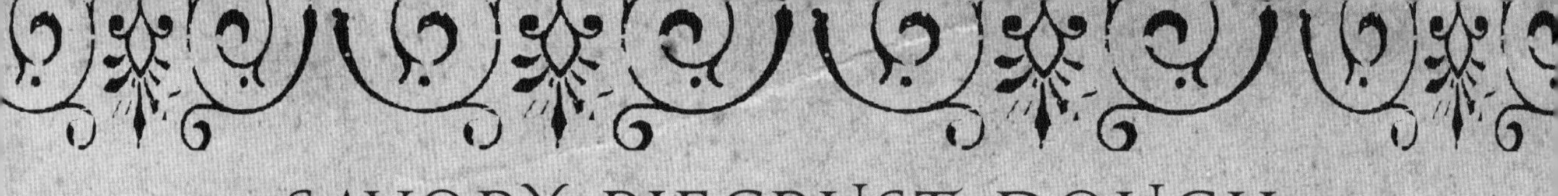

SAVORY PIECRUST DOUGH

MAKES ONE 8-TO-9-INCH BOTTOM OR TOP CRUST

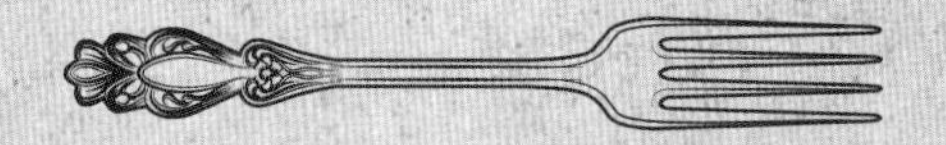

INGREDIENTS

1¼ cup all-purpose flour
1 tsp sugar
½ tsp salt
½ cup butter, chilled and diced
3–4 Tbsp cold water

It seems there is not a single episode of *Poldark* where someone is not eating or preparing a savory pie. It might be a Mutton Pie (page 124) at the Red Lion or Demelza making a Steak and Kidney Pie (page 122) at Nampara for Ross. Savory meat pies were popular for the simple reason that they were easy and cheap to make. The filling for a savory meat pie came from whatever was in the kitchen—beef, chicken (fowl), pork, or lamb (mutton), as well as vegetables that were in season.

The one constant when it came to meat pies was the crust. It was a rich and flakey crust, which was also fast and simple to make. All savory meat pies had a bottom crust, but only some had a top crust; those that didn't usually had a topping of mashed potatoes.

STEPS

1. In a medium bowl, whisk the flour, sugar, and salt.
2. Add the butter and, using a pastry blender, cut the butter into the flour until the texture is crumbly.
3. Stir in the water to form a dough.
4. Place the dough onto a floured surface and knead just until it comes together.
5. Form the dough into a ball, wrap in plastic wrap, and chill until ready to use.

TATTIE CAKE

SERVES 8

INGREDIENTS

- Savory Piecrust Dough (page 126)
- 14 oz Yukon Gold potatoes, thinly sliced
- 1 medium onion, thinly sliced
- ½ lb Huntsman cheese, grated
- 2 tsp fresh thyme
- Salt and pepper, to taste
- ½ cup chicken stock
- ¾ lb bacon (not thick cut)

Potatoes are one of the most consumed vegetables in the *Poldark* series. In season three, when Ross informs Demelza about a dinner party they are going to, she expresses excitement because she can't bear to eat one more bite of a tattie cake at home.

Potatoes have been grown in Cornwall since at least the 1700s. Since this abundant and inexpensive crop had a long shelf life and could be grown throughout the year, it made for a nutritious meal for many residents. In Cornwall, potatoes go by many different names—*tiddy*, *tetties*, *tates*, *taty*, and *tattie*, to name a few.

Tattie cake, or potato cake, is a plate pie made with a lard pastry, sliced potato, and bacon. We add some traditional English cheese and onions to our version.

STEPS

1. Preheat oven to 375 degrees.
2. In a deep-dish pie plate, prepare the dough to fully cover the pie plate.
3. You will be creating two layers of potatoes, onion, cheese, and thyme. Separate these four ingredients in half. Place a single layer of potatoes, onions, cheese, and thyme. Repeat with the second layer. Salt and pepper to taste.
4. Pour chicken stock over the completed layers.
5. Make a "lid" of bacon strips. You can arrange them in a basket weave pattern or just layer them over the top.
6. Place the pie plate on a baking pan to avoid any spillage. Cook for 50 minutes.
7. Remove from oven, let rest until slightly cool, and then serve.

 **Note:** If you cannot find Huntsman cheese, replace it with half Cheddar and half Stilton.

ALE-BATTERED FRIED FISH

SERVES 4

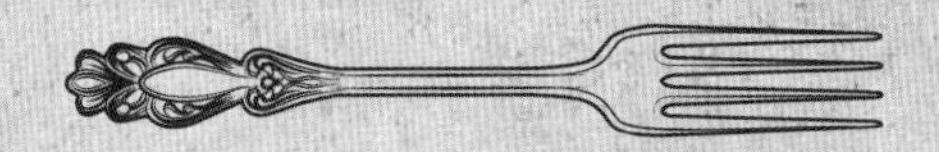

If you have ever ventured into any pub in the United Kingdom, you will probably have eaten real fish and chips. During the era of *Poldark*, boardinghouses, such as the Red Lion, were known for serving up fried fish, and their love of (homemade) ale led to the creation of a fish batter featuring their favorite brew.

INGREDIENTS

1 cup all-purpose flour
2 tsp salt
1 tsp ground black pepper
1 12-oz bottle ale
2 tsp mustard
Lard or vegetable oil, for frying
2 lb whitefish fillets

STEPS

1. In a large bowl, whisk the flour, salt, and pepper.
2. Stir in the ale and mustard to form a batter.
3. In a large skillet, heat enough lard or oil to deep-fry the fish to 350 degrees on a deep-fry thermometer.
4. Dip the fillets into the batter to completely coat. Carefully place into the hot oil or lard and fry until golden.
5. Remove the fish to a wire rack to drain of any excess oil. Let cool slightly before serving.

Note: For this recipe, use a fish of your choice, but you do want it to be a rather fleshy whitefish; any type of fish that is not fleshy will break down while being fried. When this was made in the eighteenth century, the fish was fried in animal fat (lard). Today, you can use a vegetable or peanut oil (though lard would still be preferred!). If you cannot find a good quality ale at your market, use beer.

BUTTER-POACHED COD IN A SPINACH BROTH

SERVES 4

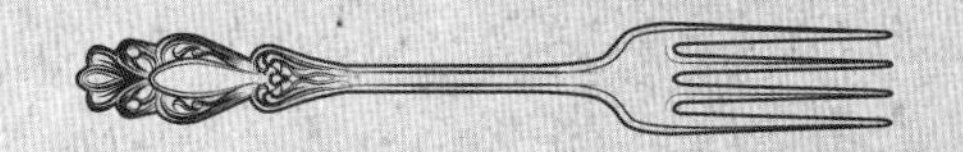

INGREDIENTS

- 2 Tbsp olive oil
- 1 cup carrots, peeled and chopped (about 1–1½ carrots)
- ½ cup sweet onions, chopped
- 2 cloves garlic, minced
- 1½ cup baby spinach
- 2 cups chicken stock
- 12 mussels, rinsed and cleaned
- 8 Tbsp butter, unsalted
- 1 lb cod fillets, cut into 4 even pieces
- ½ cup oyster mushrooms, chopped
- Salt and pepper, to taste

In season two, Demelza sets out in true Demelza form to go fishing even after Ross objects, considering she is nine months pregnant. When Prudie tries to stop her, Demelza questions how else the family is going to eat!

Defiantly, she heads out to sea in the small boat at Nampara Cove. The scenery is beautiful, the bright sky lit against a dark ocean. Unfortunately—spoiler alert!—Demelza's trip would come to an abrupt end as she goes into labor. In a classic *Poldark* scene, Ross finds her in the boat and carries her home to give birth to their son, Jeremy.

This recipe is inspired by this iconic scene.

STEPS

1. Swirl the olive oil in a deep sauté pan, on medium heat.
2. Add the carrots, onions, and garlic, cooking until they can be pierced easily with a fork.
3. Stir in the spinach, quickly sautéing, followed by the chicken stock. Turn the heat up to medium-high.
4. Once the stock boils, stir and add the mussels on top, and cover immediately. Cook for 5 minutes. Uncover. Remove the mussels from the pan and the meat from the shells. Discard the shells and set the seafood aside.

5. Turn off the heat and remove the pan off the stovetop to cool. Once the stock and vegetables have cooled, pour into a blender and mix until fully pureed.
6. Pour the puree through a fine mesh sieve back into the sauté pan. Use a wooden spoon to gently press on the vegetables to get as much liquid as you can in the pan. Discard the solids left in the sieve.
7. Turn the pan back on to medium heat and reduce the broth by half.
8. While the broth is cooking, prepare the cod. In a deep saucepan, melt the butter on medium-high heat.
9. Once the butter melts and is hot, add the fish to the pan. Using a spoon, continue to pour the butter over the fish until it cooks; you can also gently flip the fish over, but only do this once as the flaky fish will break apart.
10. As the fish begins to firm, add the mushrooms and mussels to the butter and fish. Once the fish cooks, turn off the heat.
11. Pour the broth into 4 bowls, and add the fish, mussels, and mushrooms. Salt and pepper to taste.

CHANNEL FISH CAKES

Serves 4

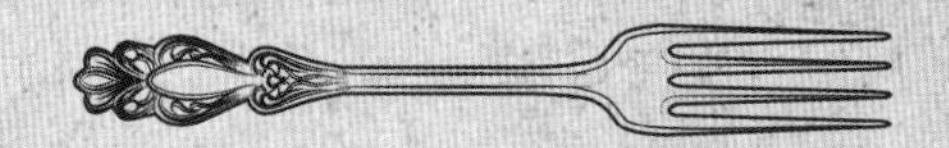

INGREDIENTS

4 cups water
2 bay leaves
5 sprigs fresh thyme
4 juniper berries
1 lb whitefish
2 Tbsp butter
2 stalks celery, minced
1 onion, minced
1 Tbsp mayonnaise
2 eggs, beaten
2 tsp salt
½ tsp ground black pepper
1 cup fresh bread crumbs
¼ cup oil or lard
Dollop sour cream, crème fraiche, or tartar sauce

While most people think Cornwall sits only on the Atlantic Ocean, the fact is the entire southern coast sits on the English Channel, which is where the fish used in Cornish dishes come from. It was much easier for local fishermen to cast a net in the Channel than the often-raging surf of the Atlantic Ocean.

Fish cakes were an important food staple in eighteenth-century Cornwall. Fish was readily available and the other ingredients required to make these delicious, savory cakes were usually in the pantry or the garden. The most common fish of the day were pilchards (like a sardine) or herring. For use in today's kitchen, you can use any type of fleshy whitefish. P.S. Don't use jars of pickled herring unless you want something that tastes truly horrible.

STEPS

1. Bring the water to a boil over high heat. Add the bay leaves, thyme, juniper berries, and whitefish. Lower the heat to a simmer and cook for about 10 minutes (depending on the type of whitefish).
2. Remove the whitefish to a plate and set aside. Discard the water and solids.
3. In a small skillet, melt the butter over medium heat. Add the celery and onion and cook for 5 minutes.
4. In a large bowl, stir together the cooked celery and onion along with the mayonnaise, eggs, salt, pepper, and bread crumbs.

5. Using two forks or your fingers, flake the fish. Stir the fish into the mixture just until combined.
6. Form the mixture into four fishcakes. Wrap in plastic and chill for about 30 minutes.
7. In a large skillet, heat the oil over medium heat.
8. Add the fish cakes to the skillet and cook, 5 minutes per side (depending on their thickness).
9. Remove to serving plates and serve with a dollop of sour cream, crème fraiche, or tartar sauce.

MUSSELS IN ALE

SERVES 4

INGREDIENTS

2 lb mussels
6 Tbsp butter, unsalted; divided
1½ cup onions; diced
4 cloves garlic, sliced
8 oz beer (we used Stella)
1 Tbsp fresh tarragon, finely chopped
2 Tbsp fresh chives, finely chopped
¼ cup fresh flat-leaf parsley, finely chopped
¼ cup Madeira wine
Pinch salt
Crusty bread, to serve

Mussels are among the most abundant seafood options in Cornwall. In the first season, Ross is walking through the seaport in Truro, attempting to secure investors for his mine. In the background, a large bushel of mussels is being sold by a street vendor.

Adding beer or ale to our recipe seemed like the perfect choice, considering that the beverage is served at The Red Lion Tavern, which is just a short walk away from the seaport.

STEPS

1. Rinse and stir the mussels under cold, fresh running water. For any mussels that do not close after rinsing, tap their shells or lightly squeeze them while running under the water again. Throw out any mussels that do not close, as it is a sign that they might not be safe to eat.
2. Melt 2 Tbsp butter in a deep pan on medium heat. Add and sauté the onions and garlic, cooking until soft.
3. Add the mussels to the pan, followed by the beer. Cover and turn the heat up to medium high for 5–7 minutes. Shake the pan periodically to move the mussels around instead of opening the lid and releasing the steam.
4. Once the mussels open, you are ready to proceed. Remove the lid, lower the heat to medium, and add the remaining 4 Tbsp butter (cut into pats) and herbs. Stir to coat all the mussels.

5. Once the butter has melted, remove the mussels with a slotted spoon and place in a deep bowl. Lightly tent with aluminum foil.
6. Keeping the juices in the pan, turn the heat back up to medium-high and add the Madeira wine along with a pinch of salt. Stir and reduce the liquid for 3 minutes.
7. Remove the pan from the heat. Remove the aluminum foil from the mussels. Pour the sauce from the pan over the mussels.
8. Do not forget to serve with a loaf of crusty bread to sop up the juices.

SALMON AND WHIPPED TURNIP PIE

MAKES 1 PIE

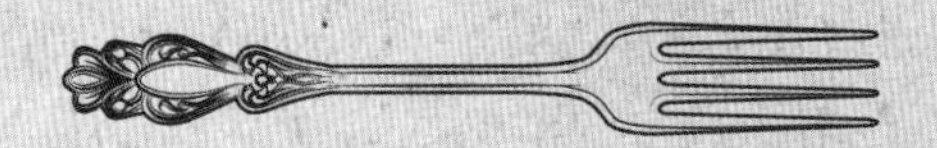

In addition to the abundant saltwater seafood, the Cornish also enjoy having access to freshwater fish. Salmon swim up to Bodmin Moor to spawn and then work their way throughout the tributaries.

This pie is inspired by an old European salmon pie recipe and the many fish pie recipes you can find in cookbooks dating around the time of *Poldark*, like the *London Art of Cookery*.

INGREDIENTS

POACHED FISH:

1 cup water
3 cups sauvignon blanc
1 carrot, sliced
1 rib celery, sliced
½ medium onion, quartered
½ lemon, quartered
4 sprigs fresh thyme
1½ lb salmon fillet
Salt and pepper, to taste

PIE:

4 Tbsp butter, unsalted; divided
2 cloves garlic, minced
4 leeks; cleaned, trimmed, green removed, and sliced into ½-inch rings
1 egg, large and whisked
1 cup plus 4 Tbsp heavy cream
2 tsp salt, divided; plus more for seasoning
1 tsp white pepper, plus more for seasoning
1 tsp ground coriander
2 Savory Piecrust Doughs (page 126)
½ rutabaga, peeled and cut into 1-inch pieces (about 3 cups)
1 russet potato, peeled and cut into 1-inch pieces
1 egg white, large

STEPS

1. Prepare the poached fish. In a medium saucepan, combine all the poaching ingredients but the salmon, salt, and pepper. Heat on medium-high until the liquid begins to boil.
2. Season the salmon with salt and pepper. Gently lay the salmon fillets into the liquid. Lower the heat to medium and cover. Depending on the thickness, the salmon should be cooked in 5–8 minutes.
3. Remove the salmon, place into a bowl, and cool. Remove and discard the skin and flake the salmon with a fork. Discard the poaching liquid.
4. Prepare the pie. Melt 2 Tbsp butter in a sauté pan on medium heat. Add the garlic followed by the leeks and sauté until soft. Remove from heat and cool.
5. In a large mixing bowl, combine the salmon, whole egg, 1 cup heavy cream, 1 tsp salt, pepper, and coriander. Then, add the cooled garlic and leeks. Gently incorporate.
6. Roll out dough on a floured surface—one piece for the crust and one piece for the lid. Grease and line a deep-dish pie plate with one piece of dough.
7. Preheat the oven to 350 degrees.
8. Fill a large saucepan with salted water and bring to a boil on medium-high heat. Add rutabaga and potatoes and cook until the vegetables can be pierced with a fork. Remove vegetables from the pan and drain.
9. Whip the cooked rutabaga, potatoes, remaining 2 Tbsp butter, remaining 4 Tbsp heavy cream, and remaining 1 tsp salt in a blender until smooth.
10. In the prepared pie plate, pour the salmon mixture into the crust, followed by the whipped vegetables, and cover with the second pie dough for the lid. Seal the pie by pinching the dough around the rim.
11. Brush the egg white on top of dough.
12. Put in the oven and cook for 30 minutes or until golden.

CHESTNUT SOUP

Serves 4

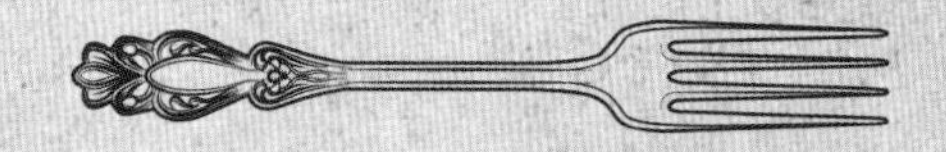

INGREDIENTS

1 lb chestnuts
2 Tbsp butter
1 onion, peeled and minced
1 potato, peeled and minced
2 stalks celery, minced
4 cups chicken stock
⅛ tsp ground cloves
½ tsp salt
¼ tsp ground black pepper
1 tsp minced thyme

If you have ever been to Cornwall, England, you know there is usually a chill in the air. This chill turns to an often-bitter cold during the winter months. During the time of *Poldark*, just like today, a bowl of hearty soup is all that is needed to warm both the body and soul. Among the favorite soups were chowders and cream-based varieties—and during the holiday season when chestnuts were available, chestnut soup would often be simmering in the hearth.

Even though it is a cream-style soup, there is no cream. The creaminess comes from the potatoes after the soup has been pureed. During Georgian times, food was pureed using something akin to a food mill. Today, you can use your food processor.

STEPS

1. Cut a shallow cross on the bottom of each chestnut. Drop the chestnuts into a pot of boiling water and cook for about 1 minute.
2. Remove the chestnuts and let cool until safe to handle. Peel off their shells and discard the shells.
3. In a medium saucepan, melt the butter over medium heat. Into the saucepan, add the onion, potato, and celery, and cook for 5 minutes.
4. Add the chestnuts and cook for 5 minutes.
5. Stir in the chicken stock, cloves, salt, and pepper, and bring to a boil. Reduce the heat to a simmer and cook for 20 minutes.
6. Spoon the soup into a food processor and puree. Pour the soup back into the saucepan and heat a few minutes.
7. Ladle into bowls, top with some thyme, and serve.

Note: While most of us think of "chestnuts roasting on an open fire," in the case of this soup, we are first going to boil them to remove the shell.

CORNISH CABBAGE AND POTATO SOUP

Serves 4

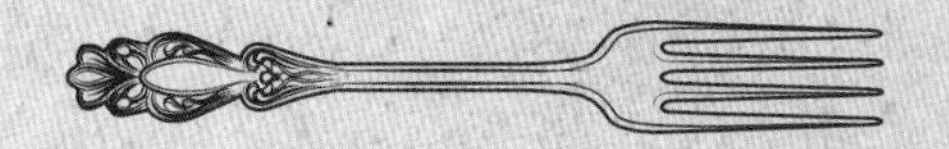

You'll truly experience the adage "bone-chilling cold" when you're on the shores of Cornwall during the winter months. Now, imagine if you lived there during a time of no electricity or heating (aside from fireplaces and hearths). Luckily, nothing warms the mind, soul, and stomach quite like a good soup!

Hearty soups were a mainstay at Nampara. In many of the episodes, you will either see Demelza or Prudie preparing such a soup over the open hearth. The ingredients for these soups often came from their own homestead, which proves one thing—the modern term "farm-to-table" was never more evident than during the eighteenth century.

INGREDIENTS

- 3 Tbsp butter
- 1 head green cabbage, core removed and leaves shredded
- 1 onion, chopped
- 2 carrots or parsnips, peeled and chopped
- 8 cups chicken stock
- 2 Tbsp minced dill
- 2 potatoes, peeled and diced
- 1 tsp salt
- 1 tsp ground black pepper

STEPS

1. In a large saucepan, melt the butter over medium heat. Add the cabbage, onion, and carrots, and cook for 10 minutes.
2. Stir in the chicken stock and dill, and bring to a boil. Reduce the heat to a simmer and cook for 15 minutes.
3. Add the potatoes, salt, and pepper, and cook for 25 minutes.
4. Ladle into bowls and serve.

LAMB NECK AND BARLEY SOUP

SERVES 4

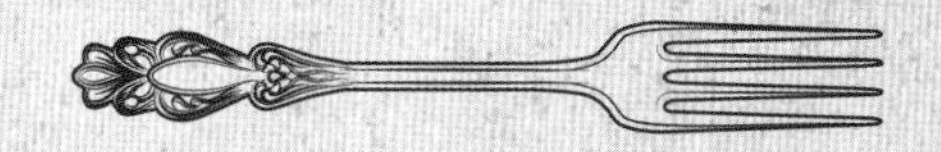

INGREDIENTS

1 Tbsp lard
2 pounds lamb meat chopped
1 onion, peeled and minced
¼ cup barley
2 carrots, peeled and chopped
2 parsnips, peeled and chopped
1 sweet potato, peeled and chopped
1 bunch kale, chopped
6 cups beef stock
1 tsp salt
½ tsp ground black pepper
4 sprigs fresh thyme

Nothing went to waste in an eighteenth-century kitchen, including the bones that were made into stock (long before today's modern fad of bone broth). You will find some interesting uses for unique parts of butchered animals that may not convey to you the idea of an appetizing dinner, such as lamb neck, featured in this soup, which is very tender. You might have a hard time finding lamb neck today, but you can use any cut of lamb meat and still enjoy this soup in all its historical glory.

Vegetables that were in season also featured in this soup, the most popular being carrots, parsnips, potatoes, sweet potatoes, and green leafy vegetables such as kale or spinach.

STEPS

1. In a medium soup pot, melt the lard over medium heat. Add the lamb meat and cook for 10 minutes.
2. Add the onion and barley, and cook for 2 minutes.
3. Add the carrots, parsnips, sweet potato, and kale, and cook for 2 minutes.
4. Stir in the beef stock, salt, pepper, and thyme, and bring to a boil. Reduce the heat to a simmer and cook for 35 minutes.
5. Ladle into bowls and serve.

CORNISH CRAB SOUP

SERVES 6–8

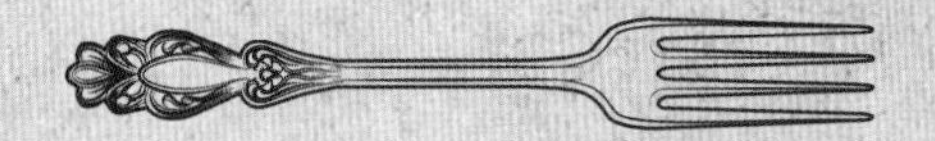

Crab, like other shelled seafood, can be found right off the shores of Cornwall in the shallow waters. Like the vegetable staples turnip and potatoes, the residences in the time of Poldark would have survived on what came from the sea—pilchards, of course, as well as mussels, crabs, and lobsters.

In the cookbook *London Art of Cookery* (1811) as well as *The Art of Cookery* (1747), there are multiple recipes for crab soup. We've used the ingredients that would have been accessible to the Cornish.

INGREDIENTS

- 4 Tbsp butter, unsalted and divided
- 1 sweet onion (about 1½ cups), halved and thinly sliced
- 2 cloves garlic, minced
- 1 carrot, peeled and sliced
- 1 rib celery, thinly sliced
- 1½ cup (8 oz) oyster mushrooms, sliced
- 1½ tsp salt, divided
- 1½ tsp pepper, divided
- 2 Tbsp flour
- 5 cups chicken stock
- 3 cups whole milk
- 24 oz baby Yukon gold potatoes; 8 potatoes halved and the others diced
- 4 sprigs thyme
- 16 oz crabmeat
- 1 cup heavy cream
- 4 Tbsp sherry
- ⅛ tsp nutmeg

STEPS

1. In a Dutch oven, melt 2 Tbsp butter on medium heat.
2. Add the onion, garlic, carrot, celery, oyster mushrooms, 1 tsp salt, and ½ tsp pepper. Cook until soft.
3. Sprinkle flour over vegetables, stir often, and cook for 2 minutes.
4. Pour a small portion of the chicken stock into the pan to mix with the flour. This will help prevent lumps. Once stirred completely, pour the rest of the chicken stock, followed by the milk, into the pan.

5. Add the potatoes (halves and diced pieces) to the pan and raise the heat to medium-high. Gently boil until the fork-tender.
6. Lower the heat back to medium. Remove the 16 potato halves and add to a blender. Pour in a cup of the broth from the pan, along with the remaining 2 Tbsp butter. Blend until smooth and pour the contents back into Dutch oven. This will add a thickness to the soup.
7. Add the thyme, crabmeat, heavy cream, sherry, nutmeg, and remaining ½ tsp salt and 2 tsp pepper.
8. Lower heat to a simmer and allow flavor to meld, about 1 hour.
9. Ladle into bowls and serve. As with any soup, this always tastes better the next day, but it also tastes good on the day it is made.

CORNISH CREAM OF MUSHROOM SOUP

SERVES 4

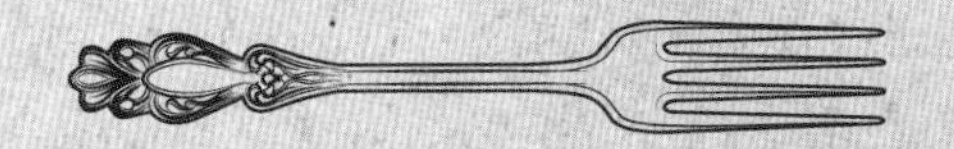

INGREDIENTS

3 Tbsp butter
6 scallions, minced
1 Tbsp all-purpose flour
3 cups chicken stock
1 lb mushrooms, chopped
¾ cup heavy cream
½ tsp salt
¼ tsp ground black pepper

Due to its climate and geographical location, Cornwall and its surrounding areas are perfect for foraging fungus—mushrooms. Many times during the show, you will see the villagers out and about with baskets, gathering locally grown food items, which tend to be mushrooms. The mushrooms used in soups were usually the older ones on the verge of drying out, which yielded more flavors.

You can use any variety of mushroom to make a Cornish Cream of Mushroom Soup. If you're looking for mushrooms at the local store, do as Demelza would do—buy the cheap ones and make something delicious!

STEPS

1. In a medium saucepan over medium heat, melt the butter.
2. Add the scallions and cook for 3 minutes. Stir in the flour and cook for 1 minute.
3. Remove the saucepan from the heat and whisk in the chicken stock until smooth.
4. Place the saucepan back onto the heat and stir in the mushrooms until the soup comes to a boil. Reduce the heat to a simmer and cook 10 minutes.
5. Stir in the cream, salt, and pepper, and bring to a simmer.
6. Ladle into bowls and serve.

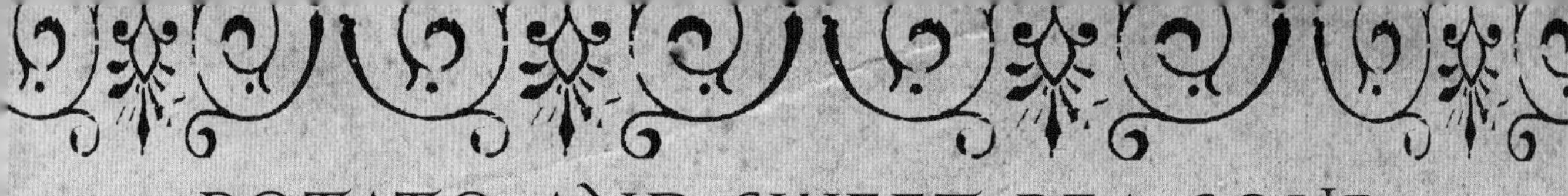

POTATO AND SWEET PEA SOUP

Serves 4

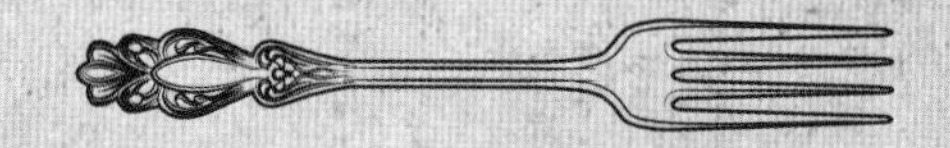

INGREDIENTS

- ¼ cup butter
- 2 onions, peeled and thinly sliced
- 1 tsp salt
- 2 potatoes, peeled and diced
- 4 cups chicken stock
- 2 cups sweet peas
- 1 tsp ground black pepper

If you have ever had the opportunity to taste sweet peas fresh from your garden, you'll know that these little green gems are the vegan equivalent of candy, and they bring a wonderful natural sweetness to a soup.

Though you may have had a "creamed" version of this soup at some point in your life, this one is a little different. Neither the potatoes nor the peas will be pureed; they will be in little chunks or whole, in the case of the peas. This soup would be served at the Red Lion Boardinghouse along with a loaf of Brown Soda Bread (page 84). If sweet peas are not in season, the frozen variety will work just as well.

STEPS

1. In a medium saucepan, melt the butter over medium heat. Add the onions and cook for 10 minutes.
2. Stir in the salt, potatoes, and chicken stock, and bring to a boil.
3. Reduce the heat to a simmer, cover, and cook for 30 minutes.
4. Add the sweet peas and pepper, and cook, uncovered, for 10 minutes.
5. Ladle into bowls and serve.

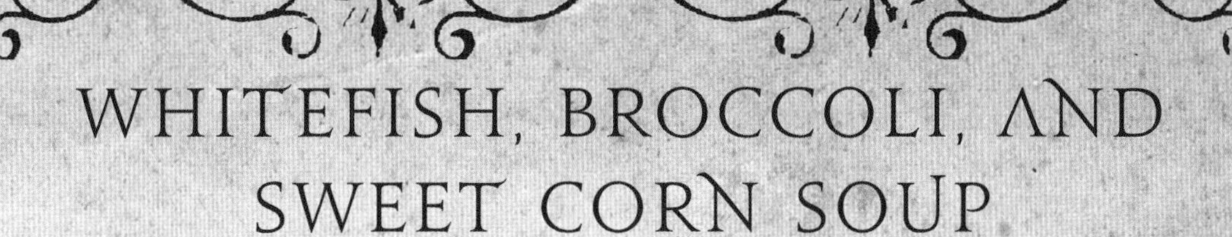

WHITEFISH, BROCCOLI, AND SWEET CORN SOUP

SERVES 4

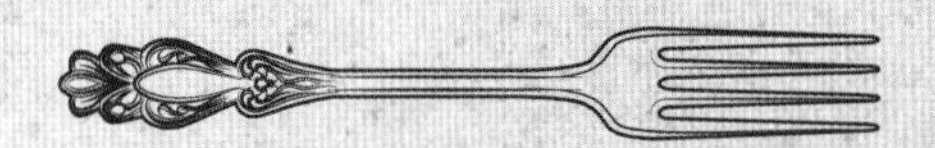

INGREDIENTS

- 3 potatoes, peeled and diced
- 2½ cups milk
- 2¼ cups fish stock
- 1 lb whitefish, cut in large chunks
- 1½ cups chopped broccoli
- 2 cups sweet corn kernels
- ½ tsp salt
- ¼ tsp ground black pepper
- 2 scallions, minced

Who had the tastiest food during the *Poldark* era—the rich (the Warleggans of Trenwith) or the poor (the Poldarks of Nampara)? This soup, loaded with flavor, was popular among the villagers as all the ingredients could essentially be obtained for free via fishing or gardening, and it rivaled any soup that would have been served in the oak dining room of the manors.

You can use any whitefish, preferably the more fleshy varieties such as haddock or pollock, both of which can be found in the fish section of most markets. The real secret to the soup's incredible flavor is what the cooks did with the sweet corn—after they removed the kernels, they scraped the cobs, which released sweet corn milk.

STEPS

1. In a medium saucepan over medium heat, combine the potatoes, milk, and fish stock. Bring to a boil. Reduce the heat to a simmer and cook for 10 minutes or until the potatoes become fork tender.
2. With a fork, mash about a quarter of the potatoes in the soup.
3. Into the soup, stir in the whitefish and broccoli and cook for 5 minutes.
4. Scrape the corn kernels. Stir in the sweet corn, salt, pepper, and scallions, and bring to a simmer.
5. Ladle into bowls and serve.

Note: If sweet corn is not in season, the frozen or canned variety can be used (but you won't get the sweet corn milk).

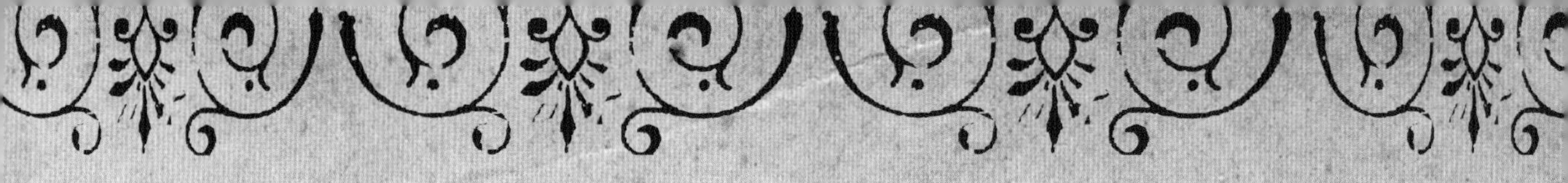

SWEET POTATO AND CARROT SOUP

SERVES 4

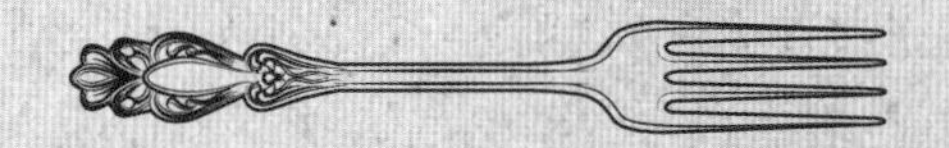

INGREDIENTS

- 2 sweet potatoes, peeled and diced
- 4 carrots, peeled and diced
- ¼ cup butter
- 1 onion, peeled and minced
- ¼ tsp ground cinnamon
- ⅛ tsp ground nutmeg
- 3 cups chicken stock
- ¼ cup honey
- 1 cup heavy cream

There is an adage that goes, "From the earth you will get life," and it perfectly describes this soup. The two main ingredients do indeed come from the earth, and after one delicious sip, you'll realize why this soup is as popular today as it has ever been.

There are two ways you can prepare this, and both ways were followed during the eighteenth century. You can either use sweet potatoes and carrots left over from other meals, or you can simply boil the sweet potatoes and carrots as outlined in this recipe. A third way will add more rustic flavor, though it was not done during this time: roast and then puree the sweet potatoes and carrots.

STEPS

1. Into a large pot of boiling water, add the sweet potatoes and carrots and cook until fork tender. Drain the sweet potatoes and carrots and set aside. Discard the cooking liquid.
2. In a medium saucepan, melt the butter over medium heat. Add the onion, cinnamon, and nutmeg, and cook for 5 minutes.
3. Stir in the chicken stock and honey, and cook for 10 minutes.
4. Place the sweet potatoes and carrots into a food processor and puree. Whisk the pureed sweet potatoes and carrots into the soup and bring to a simmer.
5. Whisk in the heavy cream and bring back to a simmer.
6. Ladle into bowls and serve.

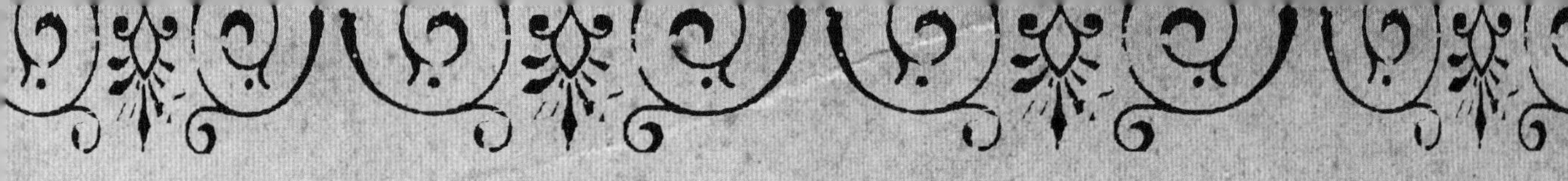

CHEDDAR, ONIONS, AND MUSHROOMS

Serves 4

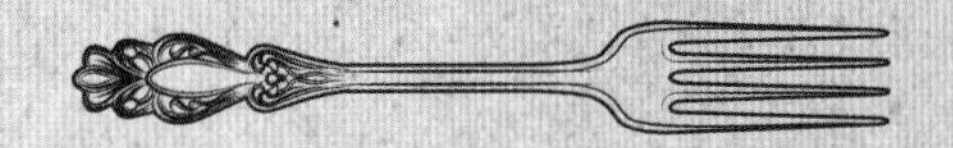

INGREDIENTS

- ¼ cup butter
- ¼ cup all-purpose flour
- 1½ cups milk
- 1 cup grated Cheddar cheese, divided
- ½ lb mushrooms, cleaned and thinly sliced
- 2 onions, peeled and thinly sliced
- ¼ cup bread crumbs
- ½ tsp salt
- ¼ tsp ground black pepper

There was one certainty when food was put on the table at a boardinghouse or homestead: it was going to be delicious and hearty. When you are not among the wealthy (or your last name isn't Warleggan), you must make do with what you have—and these people had a garden of fresh vegetables and herbs, and they made their own cheese.

Cheddar, Onions, and Mushrooms was a very common dish at the dinner table. Though it would be a "side-dish" today, in the era of *Poldark* it was served as the entree along with freshly made bread. This dish was made one of two ways: with either sliced onions or immature onions (little onions or pearl onions). You can use any variety of mushroom to make this dish, but the best are the inexpensive little "button" mushrooms.

STEPS

1. Preheat your oven to 425 degrees. Lightly oil a 3-quart casserole dish or pan.
2. In a medium saucepan, melt the butter over medium heat. Whisk in the flour until smooth.
3. Whisk in the milk until smooth and creamy. Cook, while whisking, for 5 minutes. It will thicken as you whisk.
4. Remove the saucepan from the heat and stir in ¾ cup grated Cheddar cheese until it has melted. Stir in the mushrooms and the onions.

5. Spoon the mixture into the prepared casserole dish and top with the remaining cheese.
6. In a small bowl, combine the bread crumbs, salt, and pepper. Sprinkle the bread crumb mix atop the cheese.
7. Place into the oven and bake for 50 minutes.
8. Remove from the oven and let cool slightly before serving.

CORNWALL CREAMED PEAS AND POTATOES

SERVES 4

INGREDIENTS

2 lb potatoes, peeled and diced
1½ cups green peas
¼ cup butter
¼ cup all-purpose flour
2 cups milk
½ tsp salt
¼ tsp ground black pepper
¼ tsp ground allspice

You might notice a few things when it comes to the food of *Poldark*. They used a lot of dairy (butter, cream, and cheese), produce, and grains (wheat, barley, rye, etc.). The reason for this is quite simple: they made their own butter, cream, and cheese; and they grew their own produce and grains. The people who lived in Cornwall fit the American definition of "homesteaders" perfectly.

Cornwall Creamed Peas and Potatoes is a classic English dish. So classic, in fact, that it soon became a staple American holiday tradition after the recipe was brought over on the *Mayflower*. You can't really find a simpler dish to prepare, and it goes great with whatever else you might be putting on your dinner table.

STEPS

1. Into a pot of boiling water, add the potatoes and cook just until fork tender. Drain the potatoes and discard the cooking liquid.
2. Into another pot of boiling water, add the peas and cook for 5 minutes. Drain the peas and discard the cooking liquid.

3. In a medium saucepan, melt the butter over medium heat. Whisk in the flour until smooth.
4. Whisk in the milk, salt, pepper, and allspice until smooth and creamy.
5. Stir in the potatoes and peas and cook for 5 minutes. It will thicken as it cooks.
6. Spoon into a serving bowl, let cool slightly, and serve.

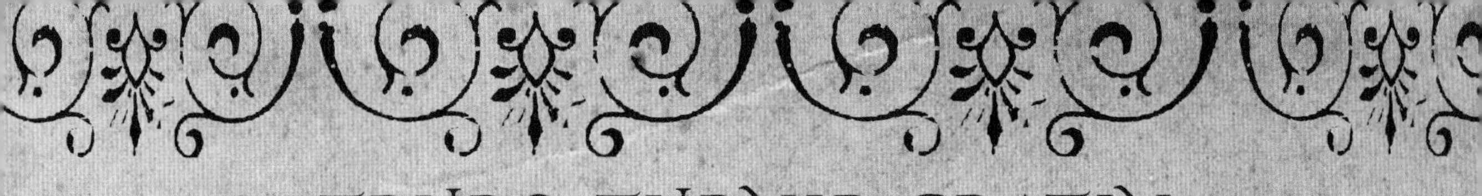

TRURO TURNIP GRATIN

SERVES 4–6

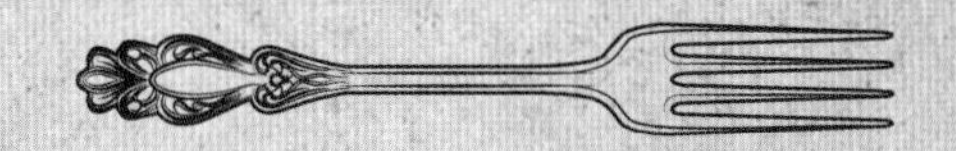

INGREDIENTS

2 Tbsp butter, unsalted
1½ tsp salt
1 tsp pepper
1 Tbsp fresh thyme
½ tsp ground nutmeg
½ lb turnip, thinly sliced with a mandolin (we used rutabaga)
1 cup heavy cream, divided
14 oz Cheddar, grated (we used a blend of sharp and extra sharp)

Turnip is one of the most common vegetables mentioned in the *Poldark* series. The root vegetable was inexpensive to grow and could feed many. It is clear what social class would eat turnips when Demelza declares, "Elizabeth was born to be admired; I was born to pull turnips," making reference to herself as low-born.

Coincidentally, local farmers in the area of Truro, Massachusetts, have also had some success with growing turnips. Surely, the town in Massachusetts was named after Truro, Cornwall, for its similarities with high cliffs overlooking the ocean, a calm and welcoming cove (Pamet Harbor), and beautiful vistas. In fact, Outer Cape Cod, where Truro is located, celebrates a Turnip Festival annually in a neighboring community.

STEPS

1. Preheat the oven at 375 degrees.
2. On the stovetop, melt the butter in a 12-inch cast-iron or ovenproof pan on medium heat.
3. In a mixing bowl, combine the salt, pepper, thyme, nutmeg, and turnip.
4. Now, lay a single layer of turnip in the pan, followed by ¼ cup cream, and ½ cup cheese. Repeat this step one more time.
5. Finally, lay on the third layer of turnip, followed by ½ cup cream, and remaining cheese.
6. Turn off the heat and place the pan into the oven. Cook for 40 minutes until golden.
7. Remove from oven and cool slightly before serving.

References

The Art of Cookery, Hannah Glasse, 2015, Dover Publications, US (originally published in England in 1747)

The Diner's Dictionary: Word Origins of Food and Drink, John Ayto, 2012, Oxford University Press, Oxford, England

The Experienced English Housekeeper, Elizabeth Raffald, 1769, England

Food History, Reay Tannahill, 1973, Stein and Day, New York, NY

Food Lover's Companion, Sharon Tyler Herbst and Ron Herbst, Barron's, 2013, Hauppauge, NY

The Georgian Kitchen, Emma Kay, 2015, Amberley Publishing, Gloucestershire

The London Art of Cookery and Domestic Housekeeper's Complete Assistant, John Farley, 1811, Scatcherd and Letterman, London

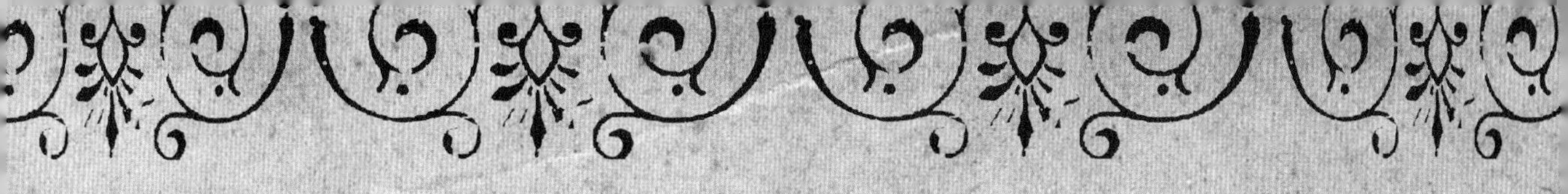

Conversion Charts

METRIC AND IMPERIAL CONVERSIONS
(These conversions are rounded for convenience)

Ingredient	Cups/Tablespoons/ Teaspoons	Ounces	Grams/Milliliters
Butter	1 cup = 16 tablespoons = 2 sticks	8 ounces	230 grams
Cheese, shredded	1 cup	4 ounces	110 grams
Cream cheese	1 tablespoon	0.5 ounce	14.5 grams
Cornstarch	1 tablespoon	0.3 ounce	8 grams
Flour, all-purpose	1 cup/1 tablespoon	4.5 ounces/0.3 ounce	125 grams/8 grams
Flour, whole wheat	1 cup	4 ounces	120 grams
Fruit, dried	1 cup	4 ounces	120 grams
Fruits or veggies, chopped	1 cup	5 to 7 ounces	145 to 200 grams
Fruits or veggies, pureed	1 cup	8.5 ounces	245 grams
Honey, maple syrup, or corn syrup	1 tablespoon	0.75 ounce	20 grams
Liquids: cream, milk, water, or juice	1 cup	8 fluid ounces	240 milliliters
Oats	1 cup	5.5 ounces	150 grams
Salt	1 teaspoon	0.2 ounce	6 grams
Spices: cinnamon, cloves, ginger, or nutmeg (ground)	1 teaspoon	0.2 ounce	5 milliliters
Sugar, brown, firmly packed	1 cup	7 ounces	200 grams
Sugar, white	1 cup/1 tablespoon	7 ounces/0.5 ounce	200 grams/12.5 grams
Vanilla extract	1 teaspoon	0.2 ounce	4 grams

OVEN TEMPERATURES

Fahrenheit	Celsius	Gas Mark
225°	110°	¼
250°	120°	½
275°	140°	1
300°	150°	2
325°	160°	3
350°	180°	4
375°	190°	5
400°	200°	6
425°	220°	7
450°	230°	8

Index

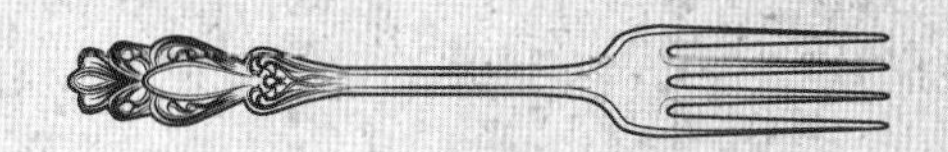

A

B

C

D

E

F

G

H

I

J

K

L

M

O

P

R

S

T

V

W

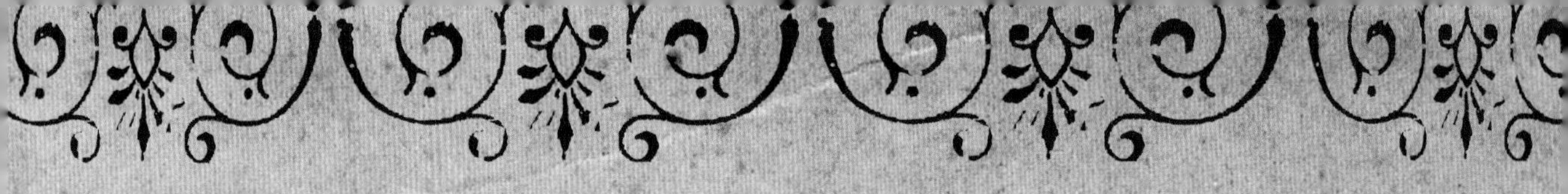